T0194129

#MIRACLEMAGNET

A Spiritual Guide To Releasing Your
Fears & Becoming A Girl Boss

AJ WILLIAMS

WESTBOW
PRESS®
A DIVISION OF THOMAS NELSON
& ZONDERVAN

Scripture taken from the Amplified Bible, Copyright © 1954, 1958, 1962, 1964, 1965, 1987 by The Lockman Foundation. Used with permission.

WestBow Press books may be ordered through booksellers or by contacting:

WestBow Press
A Division of Thomas Nelson & Zondervan
1663 Liberty Drive
Bloomington, IN 47403
www.westbowpress.com
1 (866) 928-1240

ISBN: 978-1-9736-2830-9 (sc)
ISBN: 978-1-9736-2829-3 (hc)
ISBN: 978-1-9736-2831-6 (e)

Library of Congress Control Number: 2018905581

Print information available on the last page.

WestBow Press rev. date: 07/11/2018

CONTENTS

INTRODUCTION

The Miracle Magnet

"*Love is by far the greatest gift to ever be received or given.*"

"*It's magnetic, intoxicating, liberating, and soul stirring, .*"

"*There's no one that ever ex-isted that never loved or felt
an act of love somehow, some way.*"

"*Love is the most powerful force that ever came to be.*"

"*Love is tenderness, it's devoted and unconditional and
it will forever be, until the end of time.*"

"*Choose Love*"

AJ Williams

My intention is to inspire and call you to a higher sense of inner awareness, strength and leadership. This book will help you determine whether you're a lion or a sheep and to decide which one you'll remain. Sheep are easily lead while lions are fierce and courageous. It's time to be fearless, rise up and fight back. God anoints us to take no prisoners and devour our enemies until they're no longer a threat. We must stand in full armor and slaughter them with the word thats sharper than a double edged sword. It's easier than you think if you simply trust God and give your cares to him.

He'll do all the work. You'll learn how to come through the fire without burns but rather finely polished and attract incredible miracles.

It's my sincere prayer and goal to help you curate a path to emotional greatness, spiritual fitness and physical wellness. Through my experience, and evidence in scriptures you"ll be properly equipped with the tools to harness your dreams and organize your visions. You'll get a clear and deeper understanding of who God really is and what a phenomenal life you could lead serving him.

I'm delighted to share Gods love sprinkled with battle strategies and girlfriend talk. I'm here to say that you're loved, very precious and can achieve anything, no matter how scary it may seem. This is a call to action to transform lives in the world around you while transforming your own life. You can have more than you ever dreamed possible if you only believe.

You'll also learn the power of manifesting daily miracles and increasing your finances. You'll indeed begin to fortify yourself, improve your self-care and ignite your self awareness. Most importantly you'll finally find your voice and shine your light and shout from the highest mountaintops your deepest heartfelt roars. You are steps away from becoming a miracle magnet and gaining life's most vital tools. This will empower you in winning the toughest challenges you'll ever face. So grab a cozy blanket and curl up with a warm cup of tea and enjoy.

Miracles:

An extraordinary event manifesting divine intervention in human affairs; an extremely outstanding or unusual event, a divinely natural phenomenon experienced humanly as the fulfillment of spiritual law

Finding Your Purpose

Who are you really? Have you decided? Are you still figuring it out? That's fine welcome to the club. The world is full of millions who are imperfect still trying to figure it out. We all still push through just to put one foot in front of the other, everyday. No people have perfected themselves or their lives. So there's still time for you to get it right. I've recently come to the realization that my true purpose is not to sit in silence but to stand in strength and rise to the occasion for the oppressed. To not hide and be timid but to positively and fervently contribute to humanity. To not talk about it. To not shake my head in judgement but put my talents, money and my hands where my heartfelt thoughts are.

Poverty, racism, sex trafficking, and the aids epidemic are just a few of the injustices we are plagued with globally. It's a lack of awareness, knowledge and fear that keeps us on the sidelines and in the shadows while our brothers, sisters, and family members suffer unnecessary tragedies. It cost nothing to pray or raise our voices to speak for the silenced. It cost nothing to lend a helping hand if we can. I can admit I too was blinded by the paradigm of lies that we've been programmed into by society, family history, and religion. This formulates a robotic lifestyle of being a judgmental, insensitive, unhelpful society-trying desperately to fit in, not asking questions, accepting whatever propaganda is given and going with the flow.

This is not the time to be timid. The world is in a state of dire emergency, and we can all be the change that we need.

To have a true shift in your awareness and stand firm in your belief is true freedom. This is the ultimate test of what you're made of and if you were born to be forgotten or do epic things. Once your heart is opened and your soul is stirred, you will become spiritually fit. Living consciously creates an intense and magnetic call that can't be ignored. It's a call to worship and a urge to reposition each other to win. God placed us on this planet to respect our bodies, follow christ, live well and strengthen family and friends to do the same.

At times we must call our loved ones to vibrate higher so that we can enjoy a high quality life all together. To live long, blessed and happy lives. According to Genesis 6:3, we're typically supposed to live about 120 years but that doesn't happen anymore. It's not because God went back on his word but because we've cut our own life spans by the food we eat and the choices we make spiritually. This earth is our temporary home, just like our bodies, since our spirit and soul reside within.

Your body is just a vessel to be used and operated by your deepest intentions and inner demeanor. You will only get one body, so take care of it and it'll take care of you. It'll take you wherever you want to go on this planet.

Eat, pray, love is a true analogy for a few life requirements. It's good to develop a spirit of love not only for loved ones but for your haters, and strangers alike. I know it's not always that simple, but it can be done. God commands us to operate from a loving perspective daily. Having a loving, merciful attitude towards difficult people becomes less painful after we make an honest effort; then it becomes a consistent habit.

This doesn't mean it'll be easy because of course, difficult people make things difficult. And surely they make it harder to love and forgive them. But eventually you start to see the bigger picture when you realize that operating in love is better for you-and it's what Gods commands us to do. It's bigger than your ego and your pride. It's bigger than being right and looking good.

It's about satisfying your soul and having real peace in your heart to be able to successfully move forward in accomplishing your goals.

Even when I tried to take the high road, it really wasn't the high road because I was only being sarcastic and facetious. I was trying to win and look good. We're always trying to look good in an argument or to various people. We even suffer to look good physically and to come across as emotionally strong. Some people die in sickness trying to look good by not sharing what's going on with loved ones. We want to look strong and put together all the time because the opposite is looking weak. Well, why not actually be strong and be together for real? Don't fake it, because that's the actual weakness. It shows that you're not strong enough to truly stand tall in your truth, whatever it may be. I've felt that, and it doesn't feel good. In fact it turns secret battles into agonizing realities because you've just added the pressure of hiding.

This reminds me of a time not long ago when a toxic person from whom I had distanced myself called me after a few months and said, "I thought I'd be the bigger person and call you." So I said, "Whatever" in a very dismissive way, and they immediately got defensive, angry, and argumentative. Talk about a joke! I literally laughed out loud while hanging up. I'd finally learned that the true bigger person is genuine, heartfelt and never announces, "I'm being the bigger person." Who does that? Oh, I know, people who want to look good but who haven't really changed. People who want to be manipulative and make you look small without taking responsibility.

Do you know people who constantly offend but love to flip the script and make themselves the victim? I do. Maturity is to know that making a statement requires having the ability to back it up. That's why I really don't react to people apologizing; I more or less respond to changed behavior because apologies can be rehearsed and generic. This is the reason that finding myself was an integral journey that was necessary to my survival and growth. If you learn how to master yourself, then you really learn how to master most situations around you. And if you don't know who you are, then you really don't know your next move. Your decisions vary based on perception or momentary emotions. Always keep in mind feelings can be be misleading and steal your faith.

The strength of this sort of mastery is having the natural aptitude to gage various encounters. The conclusion is your results will be more favorable than not. That's a high-level way of being, so never give your power away.

Forgiveness is not for the person who wronged or hurt you; it's for you to release the tension in your own soul. It doesn't mean the other person gets off the hook, but it means you're free from people's bondage, free from what others think and say, and free from replaying painful scenes in your mind and reliving hurtful memories.

Who has time for that? That's unnecessary self torture that serves no one but the oppressor.

> Beloved, never avenge yourselves, but leave the way open for
> [God's] wrath; for it is written, Vengeance is Mine, I will
> repay (requite), says the Lord. (Romans 12:19 AMP)

When you honestly forgive, you not only release the pain but you release the people to God for him to avenge you. Most of all, do this for yourself. Love yourself enough to increase your interest and flourish in your relationship with God. He will lift you up and meet all of your needs. God can heal emotional traumas and silence the voices in your head that want to continue to highlight your past mistakes because the enemy wants you to stay stuck. He wants you paralyzed with fear so that you don't make any sudden moves he'll regret. He doesn't want you to be delivered and developed into the wonderful and strong individual that our Father has called you to be.

Often the enemy doesn't directly talk to you because he'll get others to do his dirty work for him. He uses people in your life that's critical of your decisions and that constantly remind you of your past mistakes. He also uses everyday people to cause you strife and disruption. That is specifically designed to mess your head game up and discourage you from making any prosperous future moves. There are great things in store for you, if you just believe. So go ahead and ask God to develop your faith, increase your knowledge and wisdom, and make provision for you. Ask him to reveal who you're supposed to be in this world. You can say something like this:

> *"Lord what is my purpose for being born? Please reveal to me why i'm here*
> *and what my assignment is. How do I improve my life and the lives of those*
> *around me? I want to be a blessing and I want to live my best life."*

Not only will he show you; he'll also provide you with the tools, resources, wisdom, and people to make that come to pass. Speak and release blessings and expect him to do just that. You may say you're unsure, or you believe that your situation is different; you might have done some things you're ashamed of. Well, haven't we all?

Let's be real here, the very people who constantly gossip and gather details on others conveniently forget their own lies and mistakes. You're not alone and should consider these words I still pray everyday:

> *"Lord show me who I am. Order my steps and reveal your Glory*
> *in my life. Use me and give me wisdom to not let satan entrap me.*
> *Help me to release my past and look forward to my future."*

This is a lifelong journey of evolving and developing yourself. He will not give you talent, dreams or gifts without crafting a path for you to follow. Even if you're struggling and confused, there is nothing too hard for God. So stop doubting yourself, and stop doubting him. He can do the impossible and you can reach the impossible if you simply believe. What do you really have to lose by building your faith? The worst that can happen is that you may be disappointed if what you want is delayed. But the real tragedy is setting yourself up for failure if you lower your expectations.

Sometimes we are so fearful that we'll fail that we just expect to fail because it's easier than fearing disappointment. That's a low level thought process. It's time to indulge in some Thought Therapy and begin to reformat the way you think. Read positive affirmations in the mirror and meditate on faith scriptures. God is bigger than anything or anyone you may see as an obstacle. Open your heart and just allow yourself to dream and visualize the woman you've always wanted to be. Feel the happiness that lifestyle would bring you. Replace worry with the intensity of the things you desire the most in life.

The law of attraction is as real as the law of gravity. You attract what you spend your days and nights meditating on. Did you ever wonder and worry about something bad happening to the point that it actually happened? You attracted that. Well, that works for good things as well. Set you intention to think constantly on every good thing you desire and watch God bring it into your life. Manifestation is inevitable one way or the other.

Step 1: Ask. Release. Expect. Receive.

Side Note: Bosses Are Created Not Born Because Promotion Comes From God.

You Must Show Up To Glow Up

To get back on the road of who I was born to be and truly live in my purpose, I needed a collision. I needed to be broken, lose everything, and go through my worse storm. Basically, the old me had to die away so I could be born again and become who God truly wanted me to be.

The woman I am today is not the woman I was when I hit my rock bottom. But guess what?, I'm now the woman I always wanted to be but didn't know how to be. I regret nothing because I would not want to lose the wisdom I've gained.

Now of course I didn't feel like this soon after my worst fears came to past. But I did after the knowledge and the blessings came. I finally understood that every season has a harvest.

Every seed you plant bears fruit and there is purpose even in the things we don't understand. Rock bottom is not everyone's path, only the hard-headed ones who are stubborn, such as myself. Those who ignore warning signs that are red-hot blinking in their faces. This is precisely why the bible tells us, that the flesh must be killed in order to spiritually gain and walk in your calling. Once you start looking at the world from a spiritual perspective then you can see from a supernatural view. It's like having spiritual vision and heightened senses around normal people.

If we're not sensitive to the spirit of God, we can't hear his voice or his direction. It prevents us from manifesting the things we need. We must set the intention to curate the life we want and intensely want it. The bible teaches us to always expect good things because of our obedience. This mental shift is momentous because you now decide whether to live and fight or die and give up. This is when it will become very clear to you that low and high level living are a choice often deciding itself based on our actions.

Living and vibrating on a higher frequency is not pious, it's an intelligent choice. Your state of mind determines how you live your life and the choices you make for yourself. Your imagination is not some illusion but rather a powerful tool that should be utilized to enlist Gods best for yourself. Harness your dreams with your thoughts and intentions. In relation 2nd Corinthians 10:5 says, cast down every imagination and high thing that exalted itself against the knowledge of God and take your thoughts captive to make them obedient to Gods word.

God knows how powerful thoughts and imaginations are. I believe this is why all of our biggest and most creative dreams and ideas come through the visions of our minds. Why not use them for Christ and let God be in control, instead of letting the enemy tap dance all day in your head. Now your marching to the beat of insane thoughts of doubt and fears that contradict what our Father wants for you.

Everyone doesn't have to fall to their lowest point to transform but sometimes that's what it takes. When you're stuck in unbelief and ignore the apparent signs; you're really ignoring that gut intuition telling you to choose different.

That's when unnecessary suffering and struggles begin and of course the necessary storms will always occur. So why make the load heavier? Sometimes we create an environment of hardship that could easily be avoided with sensible decisions. It's not fun and it's a pain that can be avoided with obedience.

Pray and ask God for the answers and I promise he'll speak to your heart and guide you along the best path. This may not be what we naturally want to do but feelings are temporary. Another possibility is that, it was written before you were born, that you'll go through difficult things to develop your greatness. All to increase your plateau of faith to where it needs to be to level up. This is hard to understand in the natural world and in the midst of your trials and tribulations.

I first hand understand that emotional pain can be so intense that it develops into physical distress. I've heard legendary stories of couples being so heartbroken over the lost of their soul mate, that they died shortly after. I certainly believe it, because we're powerful beyond our beliefs. There are people who never recover from trauma leaving them with emotional and physical triggers. I've experienced agonizing heart break to the point that I felt like living was to unbearable. Why am I here, if all i'm going to do is be depressed and toil with pain and hopelessness.

Consider this, how would you know how marvelous the savior is at working miracles in a bad situation, unless you have one? Sometimes we won't change unless we're desperate enough and up against the ropes. But soon the miracles arrive and the sun starts shining again and everything perfectly falls into place. Things work out better than you could have ever imagined. That's when you'll know Gods hand is at work in your life. The revelation of why it had to happen and the blessings on the other side of the mountain will be revealed. When the miracles flow from every direction, you soon forget about the storms and vicissitudes of life. And all you're focused on is gratitude, your healing and your deliverance out of the inferno.

It happened to me. I had to renew my thinking, create a thriving living space and get rid of all negativity and doubt. I had to purge myself of my own demons and spirits of fear and anger that had attached itself to me and my family. I needed to acknowledge that generational curses are real and can be inherited. Wicked spirits are only dangerous traits, harmful habits and bad energy that need a body to operate in. It has no power without a host to control.

That's why vibes are contagious and a person having a negative aura can be felt. Have you ever been present in an environment with an angry or toxic person and they affect others to the point that now everyone else is acting crazy too? That's a transference of spirits. Now everyone's under the influence. Even the brilliant physicist Sir Isaac Newton knew this and he wasn't a known believer of christ.

However he did pay for Bibles to be distributed to the poor and served a commission to build 50 churches. He was on to something when he identified a law of energy.

"Energy is not lost or destroyed, it is merely transferred from one party to the next." — Sir Isaac Newton.

Spirits hop around and we must be keenly precautious of who we spend our time with. Especially who we sleep with, because you have sex with their body, soul and everyone they slept with before you. Ok so the act is over and everyone goes their separate ways but you may find yourself acting a certain way unknowingly. Chances are, you got up with multiple spirits of all the people you never even slept with. Now you're struggling with specific strongholds that have attached itself to your life. You're fighting a battle that doesn't even belong to you and if you're not careful; you'll walk right into your future with those connections. And if you're not spiritually rational you won't identify the sources. You must always consider and identify all behaviors and actions from a spiritual place.

Always remember everything is energy; including all relationships (chemistry) and interactions (influences). The earth is energy and the sun and oxygen are its biggest sources. Love is the earths oxygen. That's how we survive and it's not about science, physics or philosophy, it's about facts, and actuality. It's the law of the universe, it's biblical, it's spiritual and yes it's common sense too. It's easy for people to blame others for bad things that occur. Some may say well it's your fault this happened but occasionally things happen and you're not at fault. Often you can be unwillingly violated, blinded, influenced, persecuted by, and come under fire at the hands of another.

Sometimes you can't avoid unfortunate events, until you actually learn how to avoid unfortunate events. You can't avoid things completely but you'll be conscious to what's unnecessary to struggle with. You only know what you know and you don't know what you don't know until you suddenly know you didn't know it. Now this is such a significant statement and its incredibly true. You are not aware of your ignorance of things until you become aware that you didn't have that information to begin with.

This increases your options to make stable informed decisions consistently. You're no longer bound by minimized facts because you're ability to create favorable outcomes has expanded. So it's best to stay prayed up and be spiritually and financially defensive to appropriately arm yourself for warfare. Because being out of the will of God is like standing in the straight path of a Hurricane with a dead cellphone.

#Who are you going to call?
#You need supernatural covering.

It's imperative to not only acknowledge who God and Jesus Christ are, but be committed to living right and sin free as possible. No one is perfect and mistakes will still be made. But the question is, will you try and will you feel convicted if you do wrong? God is okay with the answer being yes, he loves you and he's just excited about you choosing him like he chose you.

God is so forgiving and merciful. The bible says he forgives our sins when we repent, and throws them into the sea of forgetfulness. That means it's finished and he doesn't keep bringing up your past, and every terrible thing you've done the way humans do. There's no checklist because you're brand new in his eyes. And in order to really gain the victory over your sins and not fail; you must understand what repentance is. It's not just about being remorseful, it's about a resolution to forsake your sin. You now have a beautiful, deep character to hate what you once loved.

In your heart you feel God is worthy of your praise and your obedience. With this new mindset it's not hard to do the right thing all the time, because now you're God-conscious and woke. You are always aware of his guidelines and advice. You love him so much, you never want to disappoint him. You never want Christ to feel rejected the way he felt in biblical times. It seems after all the miracles and blessings he gave, he was still rejected and ridiculed.

It's even painful for us as humans to feel that sort of hurt and shame in the natural. Remember a time when you helped someone from the kindness of your heart only to be abused and taken advantage of, then rejected?

The un-appreciation feels similar to a slap in the face. I know i've experienced that many times in my life. However i'm grateful for Jesus sacrifice and all the miracles God performs in my life daily. I'm a witness, it's not as hard as you think to serve him and obey his commandments, it's actually easy and quite liberating.

The minute I decided to stop running from my problems and answer the call to action on my life. Everything rapidly improved. I was suddenly overwhelmed with the freedom to really live my best life and feel unashamed. I no longer felt at the hands of anyone who wanted to test me or knock me down. I also stop doubting Gods love for me and I didn't fall for the fake love and adoration from others. Fake love is a manipulation tactic to disarm and subdue you. It's the number one trick that some men use against women to get you in bed.

Saying I love you to a woman is disarming, therefore depriving her of a hostile disposition.

I think it's ok to be a little hostile with certain men which only means, not being to friendly. Being overly friendly to a man can send the wrong signals and we don't want that. When you hold on to your authority, you cultivate characteristics of a boss. Let God be the center of your attention and not a man. That's when I started to win and gain the victory in every area of my life. God continuously gave me revelations and supernatural visions about who I was and where he was taking me no matter what the circumstances. He revealed the motives of people in my life. My salvation exposed men that claimed to have loved and treasured me but were really assigned to distract and derail my future.

Yes! my train was knocked off track for a minute, quite a few times but it's back on course or this book would never have been written. In fact i'd be dead if the enemy could kill me. He'd kill you if he could but his power is limited to our assistance. God has called us all to bring enlightenment to every insensible environment we enter. I know I was meant to be a world overcomer, help win souls and increase humanity in any capacity i'm able. I am called to stand among others who want to increase peace, promote physical wellness and spiritual healing. Now without any struggles or testimonies how could I speak?

Honestly I was fighting this path and literally running from God. I thought I was the last person on the planet that he could use as a change agent. In my eyes and others, I was under qualified and damaged goods - not realizing I would save lives through my stories. Honestly what would I know with no experience? I really don't mind sharing my journey if it encourages others to try a better way. I'll use my mistakes and wisdom as a guideline to fast track you to your destination while avoiding pitfalls. Ever since my childhood, I've wanted to make a difference in peoples lives. I remember being deeply affected by the tragic experiences others suffered and feeling helpless.

Although I had a brutal upbringing, I never felt like a victim and was always grateful because I knew I still had it better than most. I may have starved and missed a few meals as a child but not to the point of malnutrition or death. I was brutalized and physically assaulted daily but it made me strong and not weak. I vowed to someday rise to the occasion and let my gift make room for me. I knew my writings would remove me from poverty and afford me a better quality of life. However I didn't know how to properly channel that yearning to be great so I developed a need to please people and overcompensate.

In the beginning you feel great making others happy until you realize you're being used and its one sided. That's satisfaction for them not you, especially when you're getting the short end of the stick. There's no true purpose in trying to please everyone other than for acceptance or to feel loved. One day you'll be looking back at all those users saying, what was I thinking? They never cared about me at all. Opportunist only want you for what you can do for them and how you make them feel. Once you raise your standards, cut them off and reclaim your power. Suddenly they find fault and now they have a big problem with you.

Haters don't want you to win in life or they would never try to destroy your peace. They would have left you alone and let you be great elsewhere;

knowing they had nothing constructive to offer your life. Some people have an agenda for you, that you're unaware of. I know I thought, how could I ever think that these negative people are worthy of my friendship let alone my time. How can I want to people please so bad while ignoring the Father above who gave me life. It doesn't make any sense why we do that to him. That is who we should be concerned with pleasing. That's when you truly find your worth and the intentions of others become obvious. The truth is, longing to be accepted by people shows an even deeper unhealthy issue within. It's a sign of low confidence and lack of self awareness.

If you can't be accepted for being you and thinking for yourself, then you're around the wrong crowd. If you can't be accepted because you boldly claim a life of exalted salvation, then those aren't the friends for you. If you feel uneasy talking about Gods goodness in public, then you should rethink your priorities. If you are celibate and are dating a man constantly trying to convince you to have sex, knowing your lifestyle. That is not the man for you. When your life changes, your friends will change. You may still keep a few, but only if they're loving and respectful of your choices and love God themselves.

The true friends that God sends you will be spirit minded with a common goal of representing holiness and enlightenment. Those that truly love and enjoy your company, accept you for who your are without the gossip, side eyes and negative comments. Without trying to talk you into things that don't represent God character you can be proud of. The people in your life will act accordingly to the way you present yourself to the world and them.

These days i'm more concerned with God being pleased with my life and his acceptance. Now when I make people happy, I feel it in my soul. It's reciprocity, and a deep satisfaction that brings long term fulfillment. It's easy to donate money or give someone a dollar on the train, but those soul stirring life altering transactions will satisfy the humanity within you. It will awaken something in you, that you never knew existed. Everyday is a new opportunity to be greater than the day before and change the course of your destiny. You don't have to accept life the way it is based on your background, surroundings or genetic makeup.

This will inspire you to help in such a way that it virtually alters the trajectory of someone's life. It's quite simple, you must imagine yourself in a persons position and then have the desire to alleviate their distress. Do for them what you would want someone to do for you. Sharing the love of the Lord and leading someone to christ is the best thing you could ever do for them.

Being a witness is the ultimate gift and sacrifice. I often think to myself that the most profound thing I could ever do in life, if I never did another thing would be to share Gods love.

There's also earthly things you could do to improve a persons quality of life. Like teaching people life and business skills to put them in a position of power to support their families.

This keeps them from being dependent on this worlds systems. There are also small compassionate gestures like donating warm food or coats to homeless people so they don't freeze to death during harsh winters. This is simple but are incredible acts of love. There's also providing shelter and safety to those who are in danger seeking refuge. It doesn't necessarily have to be your home, but making arrangements counts the same. Most recently i've been advocating to stop human sex trafficking, which is a big problem not just in foreign countries but here in America.

Women and children are disappearing everyday from mostly minority neighborhoods and there's little to no media coverage about it. They're kidnapped and sold into sex slavery right here in America. They're drugged, lost and forgotten or either put to sleep and transported to multiple countries by private planes or boats. They're being hidden in shipping containers, never to be seen alive again. Especially Native American, Middle Eastern & African American women. This really affects my family and weighs heavy on my heart because my roots stem from all cultures and I have three daughters. Because this is my heritage, I've struggled with feelings that I was born into cultures of suffering and setup to fail. Then I realized God works through his people to impact others. I'm deeply affected when my activist friends tell me that while they were protesting for Standing Rock, native girls were disappearing at a rapid rate.

Why wasn't this on the news? The media didn't even want to cover the protest let alone bring light to girls going missing. Despite news trucks, helicopters and cameras out there; satan still felt he could do that and nothing would happen. What about the missing nigerian school girls and DC girls? Any single child or woman missing is a tragedy but the fact that it occurs in mass abduction and is just ignored. It reveals a deep and dark problem in our society. They tried their best to keep that off the news but yet run stories of celebrities dogs missing in the woods. There has to be a global call to change because we'll all suffer eventually. I sometimes wonder what my ancestors, who suffered great persecution are thinking. Are they in heaven looking down at this chaos? Are they wondering what will I do with opportunities they never imagined. Can they even see me from heaven or are they busy rejoicing?

Either way, I want to honor my family and those that died suffering. I don't want to waste my life and be another forgotten relative that didn't open the doors for upcoming generations.

Whether or not we realize it, our children's children; hundreds of years down the road. Are still our children. We must consider the past and where we came from and think about the future generations. The bible clearly states that we will be judged for our choices to be selfish and ignore needs when we could have helped. We must help others and not judge them because we don't agree. God has given us grace and mercy numerous times when we didn't deserve it. Mercy trumps judgement according to the bible.

> He who has pity on the poor lends to the Lord, and that which
> he has given, He will repay to him. (Proverbs 19:17 Amp)

> But if anyone has this world's goods (resources for sustaining
> life) and sees his brother *and* fellow believer in need, yet
> closes his heart of compassion against him, how can the love
> of God live *and* remain in him?? (I John 3:17 Amp)

There are disasters going on right under our noses, all while we're consumed watching reality tv shows. We must Wake Up! God commands us to give generously to the poor and speak up on their behalf before it's to late. This helps me to sleep better at night, instead of selfishly surviving. Despite my efforts, I still don't think i've done enough. I'm just getting started and with the power of God invested in me. I'm going to shake the enemy to his core and bless people as much as I can before I leave this earth.

I haven't really begun to impact the world the way I'm called to, because the way my dreams are set up- I need millions to make the kind of imprint that will create massive movements. Major changes needed to be made in my life to even begin and once I found out my network; there was no limit to the ideas that flooded by brain. God stripped me of the bad habits that I hated I had. These addictions were emotionally and physically holding me back. I was finally able to become the woman I was mandated to be before my natural birth. I admit sometimes there's a desire to be better but old habits do die hard, so fight harder. Those very setbacks will be some of the biggest barriers you've ever seen. Remember addictions don't necessarily have to be drugs or alcohol because you can be addicted to a person or even bad tendencies.

It's easy to say "one day, i'll do this or i'll be this type of person". Well that day is today! There's no better time like now, because the only way you become who you want, is by taking the first step to do just that. Once you take that first step, then boom! You're already her. Instantly that one action calls you into existence, the Queen you've always wanted to be. Now keep taking steps in that creation by being consistent and living that life for real. Be all about the life you desire and want so passionately. Do the things that the woman you want to be would do.

Always be present and clear on your dreams and goals. Taking one step, one day at a time. Keep in mind that when you're not consciously living, you are basically sleep at the wheel of life. You are fully unaware of what's going on in the world around you, right under your nose or sometimes under your own roof. You let great opportunities slip through your fingers and usually, we don't recognize the negatives sitting right next to us. It's time to snap out of that. It's time to live that fantastic life you've always dreamed of. Your glow up happens when you show up for yourself. No one will do it for you.

Life can truly become worth living on a level you have only imagined it to be. There's so much information and data out here because it's a new era. There's a shift in the atmosphere and digital technology and mental awareness has changed the game.

Stand on the mountain tops that obscure your view and roar like a raging and courageous lioness. Speak to those mountains and command them to move out of your way.

Immediately things will open up for you and you'll notice amazing truths about the world globally. You discover things about yourself that you never knew. Simultaneously realizing how phenomenal you really are. You must drown out the noise and chit chat of haters and naysayers. And see yourself through the eyes of God because no one, not even your parents can tell you who you are.

How can anyone define you and advise you of your state of being or future, when you're still growing everyday. You're still having learning experiences and constant realizations at every age and stage. How can anyone define what your reach or limitations are when they can't do it for themselves. Stop listening to others before you listen to yourself. Your creator is the only being that can read your heart and mind. He alone knows your soul and your future. Your mistakes don't identify you, it only indicates a spot on your timeline. All those times are the past, they are memories to be either forgotten or remembered. When you realize your true heritage and what you're entitled to in Christ. You'll get up, pick up the mat you've been napping on and go collect your things.

Snatch, not take because we're not being polite about it. Snatch! what the devil stole from you. Embrace the fact the the holy spirit illuminates and electrifies your very being. Nothing else matters. Suddenly all of life's biggest challenges become insignificant in comparison to the reality of your future. So what you messed up and dated a liar or had kids out of wedlock. So what you've struggled with sin. So what you've been arrested or had legal issues. Who cares if you dropped that class or your business was an epic fail. So what and so what! What are you going to do about it now? What is anybody going to do about it? Are you willing to change your life at this moment? If so, then God is here for you with open arms.

It's vital to know that when heartfelt praise and worship consume your life, false images of who you are disappear. You let go of the idea of who people think or say you are. You deny their uneducated concepts and delusions of personality. No one knows the plans God has for his people. The fact that someone doesn't want you to win in life has zero effects on the Lord blessing you. The gossipers making assumptions or conclusions about others are the very people who have not mastered their own lives.

They're hiding their own secrets and uncovered truths. They're battling demons of their own.

Believe that. That's why I've never went out of my way to be concerned with what others do because I simply don't care. Who cares what I think? God doesn't move according to others. I know i'm unqualified to read minds and hearts so I don't waste my time. It's foolish to play God and speak on things you have no true insight on, because that's pure speculation.

"Do not touch not My anointed ones, and do My prophets no harm." (Psalms 105:15 Amp)

It's best to focus on self reflection and maturing spiritually. Allow the holy spirit to guide your thought process and clear up your visions of false self identity. Those rose colored glasses disappear because your vision is 20/20. Your vigor starts emerging and you feel this incredible strength in your bones. The fear dissipates because there's no actual eminent threat of failure. It's all just the spirit of suggestion and that's how the enemy tries to control our minds. Now you're figuring out how to deal with him. It's just like working out and exercising. You don't really push through to get the final physical outcome unless you see results along the way. Those results motivate you to thrive and flourish.

This is when unexpected chances to win arrive at your door. The new you can see the benefit in opportunities of a lifetime and see the urgency of the lifetime of an opportunity. Meaning you must be wise enough to recognize very rare to normally non-existent circumstances. Involving things and events that are beneficial to you or your business. You must also realize some opportunities have a short lifespan to take advantage of. They come and go. Consequently you learn that seizing moments is an imperative and effective business strategy.

Ever heard the term we all have the same 24 hours and what you choose to do with yours is up to you? #That part. It resonates with me so deeply because I had to evaluate my own time management. I wasted more time being unproductive compared to using my time wisely. I could no longer complain about God not blessing my endeavors because I wasn't consistent. If you're not financially successful but watching Lifetime movies all day then complaining about being broke-well that just doesn't make sense.

Even when I made the biggest mistakes of my life and career, I wasn't a fan of excuses. Not even my own. As painful as it was to face myself, I did and believe me it was excruciatingly annoying. I understood excuses are only for those who make them because they really aren't beneficial to anyone else. I've always found freedom and peace in accepting my fault in things even if the chips were stacked against me and unfair. I asked myself how did I assist this person in hurting me? What choice could I have made that would've turned the direction of the situation around? What warning signs did I ignore and did I make excuses for others behaviors? I teach my children this; because it's true that taking responsibility quickens a solution and allows you a shot to take some control back.

After growing up with questionable and sub par parenting and letting that be my guide into bad relationships. I knowingly allowed people to exploit and manipulate me. Hence those days are gone and i've refused to be anyone other than my best self. I don't care what the world does. I certainly won't be a hypnotized follower of pop culture in a world that's sex crazed, image driven and has its priorities completely twisted. It's time for deliverance from that. We must be leaders in this world where witchcraft is practiced in broad daylight. It's now embraced and socially acceptable to communicate with dead spirits.

In the Bible this is considered sorcery and so is astrology and black magic. Talk to God and the holy spirit, that's the power source not mercury retrograde. Why worship the moon and stars when you can worship the creator of the entire galaxy? The Father has all the answers to life and we can read it in the Torah or the Bible.

"When you enter the land which the Lord your God is giving you, you shall not learn to imitate the detestable (repulsive) practices of those nations. There shall not be found among you anyone who makes his son or his daughter pass through the fire (as a sacrifice),one uses divination or fortune-telling, one who practices witchcraft, or one who interprets omens, or a sorcerer, or one who cast a charm or spell, or medium, or a spiritist, or a necromancer (who seeks the dead) For everyone who does these things is utterly repulsive to the Lord; and because of these detestable practices the Lord your God is driving them out before you." (Deuteronomy 18, 9-12 Amp)

#Well #OpenYourBible #IHaveNoZodiacSign

We will be accountable for our boldness, actions, beliefs, and our choices to ignore and to be silent. We will be accountable for our choice to only be concerned with our household and those we know. Will the real leaders and freedom fighters stand up? Lets celebrate individuality and a firm belief that healing is what the world needs. There's so much excellence to life even in the midst of the chaos. There is incredible freedom in releasing your God given gifts and using them to inspire and uplift. In this space there are unlimited ways to vibrate higher and live by supernatural increase. This is pure happiness and limitless joy.

There are so many people to meet, children to feed, lives to save and continents to dance across. I can't even imagine leaving this world feeling like I failed without leading a powerful life of change. I don't want to die knowing I didn't appreciate and enjoy the greatest miracles Christ offered me. Living a high life has brought unimaginable advantages to me due to a changed mind. Because when you're in sync with your purpose, everything flows without restrictions. Your words match your actions and the outside emulates your inner conduct.

You are the Truth! And it's the same way with your character, intentions and behavior, they too mirror your inner being.

We've all lost our way before but what is your resolution to challenges? Do you make them worse? I know I have. Do you remain lost and confused drifting through the debris of humanity? Been there. Are you overcome with terrifying thoughts of the unknown, failure and fear? I got a T-Shirt but I finally burned it. Your honest assessment of your profile, determines whether you're creating the life you want or are a victim of whatever happens happens. The latter is the worse place to be because you have no control in the events that take place. Your destiny will be at the hands of anyone.

To prevent this you must operate in the authority God has given you. We must do the work needed or there will be no progress in our future generations. Growth is everything, literally. With growth, you get better. You also Glow better. Learning to love myself and heal my wounds has been my greatest journey. Even healing my own daughter from epilepsy within a year of diagnosis. All while taking multiple organ-damaging medications. A doctor told me that one of the medications she was taking at 4 years old would cause peripheral blindness after about 8 months on it. I cringed but immediately took flight. I didn't allow fear to paralyze me and hinder her healing. I knew I had to act fast and call on God for total restoration and to give me the strategy to make this possible. I first stepped out on faith and took her off the meds and her wellness journey began.

This was all done with food, herbs, fasting and Gods healing power. My number one daily food ingredient was lecithin, a brain boosting fatty ingredient. I would add it to her wheatgrass smoothies everyday. I'd put chlorophyll (plant blood) in her food and in her bath. Because the skin is the fastest and most effective way to get something into your bloodstream. She went from having multiple daily brain damaging seizures to none in less than a year. However I was ill-advised to prepare for her to have this well into her 20's. I did no such thing. I prepared for the victory.

Food is very powerful and doctors don't always know what is best for you, but that's another book. I stood on faith, I prayed and expected God to heal her. I never accepted this would be her final outcome. I didn't even prepare my mind to get used to it. I did not fear and I spoke her healing into existence. I had her recite "I am healed", everyday. "God loves me and wants me healed" and she would repeat that at 4 years old.

From the moment I witnessed this miraculous power, advocating healing has provided a sense of accomplishment of something more than myself. Seeing God perform a miracle on my own child the way i've always read about him doing in the bible has blown me away. I only wish I had the wisdom and faith to do this for my baby brother who died many years ago from juvenile diabetes. I sometimes think had I not been caught up in my own young life and partying and taken a more active role. Would he still be here? Maybe I could have educated myself more, but at the time we only knew what little the doctors shared. I was busy being a young mom and trying to survive myself.

I wonder had I been conscious and smarter and more mature, could I have made a difference in his quality of life. God is the best of all planners but I did have those thoughts. One thing is for sure, I would have nurtured him more deeply. It strengthened my faith and i'm in awe of who he is and what he's capable of. I'm now extremely confident in supernatural awareness and it's wonder working power. I speak from real life experiences and I truly hope you find answers, emotional rest and self healing in this book. Let the light within you illuminate your world.

Step 2: Be Sensitive To The Holy Spirit

Side Note: Listen To The Voice Of The Lord, Not Others.

Dating Down aka Unyoked

Girl Aren't You Tired? I know I am. I had to get out of my own way and stop making poor decisions. Choices like, what I ate, my quality of friends and absolutely the men I chose to love. Actually let me clarify that I never truly chose the relationship. I was always chosen and I accepted when I should have declined. I chose to accept a convenient suitor because he pursued me. Remember you don't always have to like who likes you for the sake of dating. Being single the last 2 years has been exceptionally gratifying. I've been in consistent long term relationships since high school and i'm more successful and productive now. I see some of my girlfriends constantly repeat the same mistakes when they know better; jumping from relationship to relationship.

We're skipping the self-healing process but urgently pressing go to the next boo. We're not even allowing 3 months to a year before getting serious with the next guy. I do see myself in them and I thank God for deliverance and clarity. Often we don't give our hearts time to mend and invest in repairing the damage. Lets learn to choose better and create beautiful, healthy interactions with males. Without the later regret or beating ourselves up for not preventing heartache. If not, its the same scenario as before and when he acts up, we react with such pain and disbelief as if we thought he was going to be different than the last guy. We aren't even different ourselves and we're not choosing different.

Honestly some of us don't take the proper time to mature as women.

The pressures of society make us feel that if you don't have a man you're failing in life. Or if you're not having sex, then you're somehow invaluable as a female. This makes us feel as if, what are you here for if not to pleasure men. All lies. Propaganda clearly created to further the demise of respecting women. It's a refusal to respect us for setting standards for ourselves and living by Godly creeds. I dive deeper into this subject in my next book, Addiction to Men.

#YouCanNotChangeAMan
#OnlyGodCan

We've bought into this mass delusion that we have to be soft and submissive with no backbone to snag a man and not make them feel intimidated. As if we're afraid to be alone even for a few weeks to purge the soul ties. Often to scared to say "hey i'm taking a break, i'm celibate and I want a Godly man that loves and honors the lord". All because we fear judgement by society. We're willing to risk the sanctity of our womanhood to not feel that sting of rejection. I've met women that are so desperate to get married just to have the title of wife, despite that man not being husband material.

I myself are guilty of dealing with a man who is unfaithful and untrustworthy. I've dated men who have unethical attachments to women they keep in their lives. I've also dated men who are disrespectful and unkind to their sisters and mothers. There's something seriously disturbing about a man who constantly lies and can't be trusted pass the front door. That's unhealthy and to stressful. Not to mention the wrong man in your life is the ultimate distraction that consumes your attention. It's ok if you've been in these relationships, it's never too late to start over now. It's never too late to walk away and choose yourself. Release him sis! It's not worth your peace.

Celibacy is a lifestyle but also a level up into another realm of blessings from God. Our backbones have to be strong enough to stand tall. Standing tall and fearless, like the lioness who dares anyone take her crown. We must really be careful because there's so much at stake. When you allow somebody to enter into your life, they are literally walking into your future and your family. That can be dangerous and may not be the will of God for your life. Maybe they aren't supposed to be apart of your journey. Now you've altered your path because you ran interference in a holy plan.

It's mandatory we know what our enemy is capable of. Never underestimate your opponent; it could be lethal. He's cunning and can look like the bread and the butter to your meal. Don't bite girl. Do not take the bait, considering there's a diabolical agenda to thwart your existence. That fine and beautiful man you're attracted to may be on assignment to get you from under your covering. A seed planted to lure you away from under the royal protection of a King. Then leave you to deal with the fall out of all kinds of craziness breaking lose in you life.

Have you ever admired a woman in a relationship with a beautiful man, who's not perfect but is so incredibly loving and consistent. Then you look at your guy wondering; How? Why? Feeling stuck? Well that's what you accepted instead of being intentional and patient. Stick to your standards and don't accept anything less than the kind of man that you know will blend well with your ideas and beliefs.

The Assignment: Distract and pretend to dig her so she'll bypass her potential. Leave her undeveloped and out of Gods will.

You must close certain doors that lead to sin with men because your kingdom is at risk. Life changing miracles and blessings are at risk and your priesthood is certainly at risk. I used to sin with men, had children out of wedlock, and looking for love in all the wrong places. Treating cheaters like husbands while they were treating me like an option. I was putting peasants (players) on pedestals who hadn't even earned the respect of their own peers and family members. You would think that was a clue but... Okay! It wasn't. Moving on. These were men who were phony, living double lives and draining the very life out of me. Be very careful, satan is subtle and charming in a way that will set you up for failure while stroking your cheek at the same time. A simple forehead kiss could be sinister.

You'll be so caught up in passion and romantic sentiments you won't notice you're being setup. He'll hand you a rose with one hand while holding a dagger behind his back; and run the same lines to another woman. Ladies it's time we sharpen our own weapons of warfare and put on that full armor of God. Like most people I figured i'd only be punished for my sin if I ever went to the lake of fire one day. So right now i'll just enjoy life, do what I want and repent one day before Jesus comes back. I got time. Right? Wrong!!

You don't have time because sinning on your own is detrimental enough but sinning with a man is even worse. Now you've involved another person into the equation. You value their opinion over your own voice of reason and over Gods commands. You're insensitive to the holy spirit because your flesh is weak. I can certainly speak from first hand experience of how damaging the wrong man in your life can be. When you date an ungodly man you are basically forcing him into the plans that the Father has for you. He becomes a God in your world. This alters your flight course and has now invited turbulence because you've just switched pilots. We know better and still do it so we must find the strength to say no and stick to it.

[For being as he is] a man of two minds (hesitating, dubious, irresolute), [he is] unstable and unreliable and uncertain about everything [he thinks, feels, decides]. (James 1: 8 Amp)

Ouch! Ok lord, so you're saying if I flip flop on certain things I flip flop in all things. Well that's not cute and it seems a little weak too. I hate feeling weak. I've felt the most weak when i've given into a mans sweet talk, knowing he wasn't any good. Fully knowing he was lying through his neck and I still surrendered my mind, heart and body. When I think back on it, I feel like I willingly gave myself to a predator without using any wisdom. It was my flesh, because women have a lustful nature as well. We see what we want and ignore what we don't want to deal with. That longing to feel wanted and needed delays Mr. Rights arrival, because our time is occupied with Mr. Wrong.

Ladies it's ok to be single for a while. It's ok to love on and nurture yourself. It's even ok to desire a good man or companionship. Ask God to send you the right man while you patiently wait. What's wrong with waiting? This time could be well spent by getting your body tight- if it's not, cleaning up your credit- if need be and improving self balance as a whole. Putting yourself first and being concerned about what God thinks of you, ensures you'll be the best.

He has the authority to say yes or no to our dreams. You would think taking that into consideration would be the highest priority. Consider this, how would you carry yourself in the presence of Jesus, if he were here and could see you in the flesh? It goes without saying, we'd be on our best behavior right? Well we should be that way anyway because he's presence is here and God sees all. I used to feel like the things I was doing was invisible to him. That was me being foolish and unclear. Being a boss is always the best way to attract a excellent man. Not a good man, because that's average. We want men operating in a spirit of excellence in everything he does. Mediocrity won't do here anymore. I don't mean being bossy but showing leadership in your life. Let him see you put God first and giving yourself that extra care and attention you desire. Let him see you running your own business and staying out of mess with your girlfriends. Let him see you build an organization that provides water and power to villages and homes in darkness. He needs to see you illuminate the world by any means. You teach men how to respect you by laying the foundation of self-care. Be strong and unwavering in your beliefs and stand firm that you're not easy or indecisive. You're basically oozing the vibe of, if you're here to try, trick or treat me. I'm not the one! Push on.

I'm not here for the games, i'm here for a serious King, all dogs must report to the junk yard not in the presence of a royal Queen. Don't dare tolerate the presence of a player or a dude thats just trying to get a good woman but he's not a good man. It makes it hard for the real men of God looking for a wife. Honestly the dogs come right from choosing at the club on Saturday night to the house of God Sunday morning. Hunting for another woman different from the one he had last night. Looking for a different type of satisfaction but still the same. He's not in the temple to change or find the lord but scouting for his next roll in the hay.

That's a perfect example of a setup and a demon on the prowl to trick you out of your inheritance, because all we see is he's in a place of worship.

So he must be saved and love baby Jesus, right? Wrong. Keep in mind that demons and witches pray too. Now yes, I know it's a shame but we all know it's true. So lets be on point, use wisdom and know them by their fruits. Anyone can come off the street and walk into a building. I'm just saying in the realm of dating, don't have a false sense of security because a man goes to church or synagogue weekly.

> *You will fully recognize them by their fruits. Do people pick grapes*
> *from thorns, or figs from thistles? (Matthew 7:16, Amp)*

Take this time of solitude to find yourself, fall in love with the woman you're becoming. I'm not speaking of a simple bath. I want you to indulge in a good green luxurious detox spa bath meanwhile drawing toxins out of your skin. Buy some fancy bath bombs and luxury healing soaps; you deserve it. This will assist in your physical and mental cleanse. It's imperative to do a whole life detoxification process. Go the extra mile to give yourself the best attention and the best skincare regimens. Eat plant-based foods and fast from all flesh foods (meats) to give your body optimum performance levels. This is the ultimate system reset and detox in my opinion. You deserve the works so you can give your future husband the very best that God has. You are his best and believe it.

Lord knows it feels good to not deal with any foolishness that comes along with dating down, so be careful not to drop your crown. This is the best time to focus on yourself, infact being in a relationship with the wrong dude is to much hard work when it shouldn't have to be.

Anything from above is not going to require all that, if he's really heaven sent. That too was a lesson hard learned for me, and once I allowed God to lead me, that created a sequence of smooth ebb and flow in my life. Not perfection without struggle but it brought order and wins.

I can honestly say I'm happily celibate and I swerve men daily, literally. I, like many women around the world have been involved in abusive relationships. I looked the other way and forgave violence and betrayals to easily. So i'm in no rush to date or have sex until i'm married. I should have done this many years ago and stood for my integrity and standards.

I shouldn't have lowered my guards and left my heart unprotected. But it's never too late to give God your loyalty and demand high criteria for your time. Remember just because you've lowered the bar in the past doesn't allow others the right to make you feel that's all you deserve. We've all lowered the bar before and skirted on the borders of regret. Now that I've found and fallen in love with myself the Lord is going to have to drop this new guy from the clouds with glitter wings attached so I know it's ordained to even get my attention.

I simply mean, i'm unbothered and found a higher purpose that's more fulfilling than some guys desire to know me. I recently had a Doctor checking me out at my daughters college orientation. The moment the light banter shifted to slight interest of dinner, I hit the door quicker than ice-cream melting on a hot Texas day. Yep! that fast! When he started giving me flirty eyes I was like,Oh oh, it's time to go. Not interested and I have no time to waste. I have a business to run and I need to go. I'll admit the old me would have said, hmm, successful physician, what's the harm in dinner. But the spiritual wisdom in the new me says, his credentials need to be heavenly not earthly or professional.

Ladies, a mans car or job does not define his propriety. And just because he says he believes in God, that doesn't equal honoring Christ. It's all about character, his mindset and principles (code of conduct). These are questions to ask yourself. Does he enhance the world? Are his values in alignment with yours? Does he improve the atmosphere after he leaves? Does he pray with you? Does he make atonement for his wrongdoings? Does he honor biblical rituals? Does he honor the Sabbath? All questions and answers that change the fate of wasted time, failed marriages, relationships and broken hearts.

These are valid questions that we are terrified to ask, because we haven't wanted the answers. This is related to the terror of asking someone you want to be sexual with to take a STD check up. We purposefully overlook unfavorable aspects and let men get away with debacles of grandness in the early stages. Wisdom indicates this is just a intro of more drama to come.

Nevertheless we stay and allow ourselves to become deeply and emotionally attached. We then have children and families with these men knowing all along he was a rolling stone after the first 2 weeks.

If he cheated on you, what sense does it make that he's not a serial cheater and he'll magically become faithful in time. Maybe he'll be so devastated that you're devastated, that he'll never do it again. Although he knew it would hurt you before he did it, and he willingly did it anyway. My personal motto is once a cheater, always a cheater. If you've caught him in lies, what sense does it make that in time he'll grow to be honest. That's not how men operate and women are not stupid. In fact we're highly intelligent beings. Women are masters of brilliant minds and the choice to pursue and commit to unhealthy relationships; is an unintelligent and poor decision. It's choosing to ignore and accept a low frequency connection.

We knew what we were doing, we just decided against better judgement. Self love is the greatest love, it's very instrumental but should be considered by all women a survival skill set. Self love helps to create boundaries, goals and standards. It fortifies you to stand up for yourself and speak your truth instead of reclining in low confidence and male intimidation. Royalty marries Royalty, right?

You deserve the best. Right? You deserve a high quality man treating you like the Queen you are with the utmost consideration. Compassion is a quality that gets lost in translation between adults. You can't expect perfect behavior and you shouldn't write someone off, if they're not everything you expect. However you deserve someone who you feel is equal to your location in life. Is his mission parallel to yours?

You deserve a man who covers you in prayer and takes a firm stance as a head of household. Not as i've experienced which is men who want the power, control and recognition as a leader of a household but lack the common sense to actually run it. That's just incompetence. Why would we ever cower in submission to a coward. This leads to the potential of two cowards running a household. This is a home built on a deck of cards and not a solid foundation. Some of us don't want to admit that we've dated some cowards. Someone who's too afraid to do the right thing and not at all brave enough to keep his word. You should never submit your power just because he's a male.

Especially one who doesn't know how to pay bills, create progressive strategies for the family and most of all; he doesn't want to work and make money consistently. You can't build anything and be broke. Who's going to respect that sort of dysfunctional non leadership?

Nobody with good sense eventually. Families can't sustain on good sex and physical attraction.

We should never follow a man who doesn't follow christ since he'll only lead you into the pits. God commands us to be equally yoked, for this specific purpose. It would alleviate the pressures of not being on common ground mentally and spiritually. If this was taken into consideration beforehand, we wouldn't even make it to the physical part. There's nothing worse than the feeling of not being able to un-sleep with a man. You can't take sex back, you can't untie that soul-tie, you just made. Not without repentance and redirection.

You don't need a man who completes you, thats a myth because no man can do that. You should be complete in yourself as a woman in what fulfills your visions and dreams. Often mothers say that our children are our lives and they complete us. That may be for a short period of time when they are needy and helpless. But once they think and choose for themselves, you quickly discover that you are still unfulfilled in your own ambitions. Children can't fill those voids and you can't fill it for them. You must not forget about yourself, and it's easy to do that.

I've been guilty of catering to a man, my kids and friends. I often neglected myself and my own needs for many years. Only to feel sick about what I haven't accomplished all while seeing with my own eyes, everyone operates quite well without me. Our children are our future but never neglect yourself. Put yourself first after God or you're no good for them.

Choose you so you can meet their needs more efficiently. If you don't have children yet, this data will greatly benefit your future parenting.

Let's also talk about being competitive. There's a vast number of women competing for the same man, or just competing period. We all know that, but what about the men? Have you ever been in a relationship with a man, you felt was jealous of you? Or competing with you? I have.

I'm quite sure some of you have as well. It seems to be an epidemic if you ask me. It's the craziest thing and one of the worst feelings to have. Your man should have your back, support you and help elevate you, but instead he may want to pull you down. Any man constantly highlighting any misfortune or hurtful experiences you've had, wants to destroy you in some capacity. That is not love. A bad guy would rather overthrow the whole kingdom and destroy the relationship then stay in his place as a man; instead of switching lanes acting like a female.

Some who have failed in life and not really accomplished much, may feel insecure about your success or your drive to build a business. They may feel threatened by the brand you're so boldly creating. You may not have built anything yet, but just your sheer drive and ability to curate things from nothing to something can be intimidating to a lesser man. What about the guy who is only ambitious when you're boosting his ego but never acts on anything. We encourage him with new innovative ideas of creating a business, or even going back to school. Then he finally acts on one of your dope ideas or suggestions and now he's constantly telling you how horrible you are and how wonderful he is.

It's really hilarious more than sad. A perfect example of unyoked is to discourage your bright ideas, sow discord or instill doubt to dismantle your throne. Most often this is a power play to keep you in your place and make himself feel higher. He may feel if you boss up, you just might think you're worthy of a better man. It's the old reverse psychology trick. If I make you feel like you're beneath me or unworthy, then you won't leave me and you'll accept my bad behavior. And one of the oldest tricks in the book. You'll be so caught up in the codependency of the dysfunction, you can't gain perspective. In their minds they try to play tough but deep down they're questioning how you're even with them. Truth is, he's not good enough, but somehow we don't see it until the bird hits the fan.

Truly some men can be the best actors in the world and you never really know what's running through their minds. I never allow a man to take care of me anymore and hold all the cards.

Money is a power play over women and guys know that. When you're in need, they give you just enough to make you feel obligated and in debt. Like you owe them one and they're subject to collect anytime. Therefore it's best to make your own money and be self-made. Be very wise and learn to not listen to what's being said but be sharp in truly spotting a fake and discerning a real one.

Ask God to bless you with the gift of discernment. It will give you keen insight into things that are normally not seen to the naked eye or revealed to the sleep ones. Love is supportive, it's kind and gentle. It can coexist and mutually share ideas that tighten our bonds. We must attempt to thrive despite the disconnect, chaos or drama in the world. Love makes us strong and keeps us connected. Wait on a wonderful man of God who will love you like Christ loved the church, because that kind of love seems worth waiting for.

Step 3: Never Follow A Man Who Doesn't Follow Christ

Side Note: Don't Look Down Or You'll Drop Your Crown

God Is Not A Statue

Has A Plastic Statue Ever Had Any Power?

I'll Wait. . ..

It never has. Once you have a clear understanding of what your purpose in life is, then everything around and inside you will change. However this information is a mystery until you truly know God. Everything should be exceptional, even your struggles should be minimized but not none existent. Life won't be perfect but your new found power will translate the way you react to life's storms and issues. Instead of panic, you will resolve to pray and manifest the most favorable outcomes.

The quality of your life upgrades from mediocre to premium, upgraded living. The appendix of everlasting life in heaven is the Bonus! Now In order for that to happen, you must know God intimately. Up close and personal and not an occasional prayer where you ask for a hookup or shout him out before eating. It's crucial to include him in everything, consult with him on decisions and ideas and watch him bless all that you do. Be dedicated to spending time with him daily and weekly. Nothing worthwhile can last without knowing who he is. God is everything. The sun, the moon, energy, love and most of all the entire Universe. Of course he's the universe, he created it.

No we don't worship the universe because there is only God but we acknowledge and love it as his finest work. He created earth our home, to breed oxygen, air and water for our survival. He is everywhere and knows all things and all thoughts at the same time. God is not a statue. A statue did not create anything ever and has no power. That is a religious myth and false god created by man to divert your path to finding him. For any human to bow down on bended knee to a plastic statue is an abomination. It is an insult to the true creator of this planet and to all life forms. That is a false religion created to distract you from the true wise God. He is not a human and we humans are not Gods.

However we are a reflection of him. The bible does tell us that we are made in his image.

> *So God created man in his own image, in the image and likeness of God he created him; male and female he created them. (Genesis 1:27, Amp)*

Humanity having the likeness or image of God does not mean in the sense of deity or divinity but rulership over the earth. We are to have dominion over this world in leadership. God is a Spirit, so therefore we have clear instructions that we are here to be spiritual beings and operate our lives from a spiritual and Godly perspective in all we do. Our bodies only house our souls and we are instructed to overcome our flesh and not be controlled by it. The bible also tells us, that we have the same power that was in and upon Jesus. The provision of power has been made to you through Christ. We are to be christlike. You simply must believe and stand firm in this truth or it doesn't apply. Faith comes by hearing the word of God.

> *I assure you and most solemnly say to you, anyone who believes in Me [as Savior] will also do the things that I do; and he will do even greater things than these [in extent and outreach], because I am going to the Father. (John 14:12)*

Our conscience and mental capacity to reason socially and vibrate in our highest state sets our dominion over the animal world. The only way to communicate with God is spiritually. Once you accept his love, you are sealed with his Holy Spirit. That's how he inhabits our praise and our bodies. We give him the praise, he gives us worship. He occupies our worship with his presence. This is a perfect example of likeness in his image and is the most supreme way of living. Just living in your natural state limits your capacity to learn, grow and expand spiritually. It generates a life of struggle, hardship and confusion without authority and without protection. Surrendering to the holy spirit is living a life like none other. Now we awake to blessings and amazing possibilities not anxiety and fear of things we must face.

It creates a significant difference in the quality of life and you essentially become a Miracle Magnet. Living in nothing but unlimited potential is a superhuman way of being. It feels incredible to arise to Gods grace that renews daily. God is Love and accepting his guidance reigns victories and wins over anything you may be facing. The enemy likes to trick people into believing that being Christian or Jewish is a boring, hard life of following to many rules and rituals. That's simply not the truth. He wants you to think that God doesn't care about what you go through or want you to enjoy life.

When in fact he doesn't want you to realize the truth about what God says will be available to you if you do follow him. You're privy to wealth, abundance, blessings and unlimited supplies for your home. You're entitled to an overflow of food and favorable conditions in this earth that are being controlled by demonic powers that be.

You'll need all of these things, especially the way things are going in this world. Our planet is in a state of emergency. All sort of ungodly atrocities are taking place in every corner of the globe. This is a serious time to pray and not have our heads in the sand and be distracted by television or social media. I used to hate to watch the news because it was so depressing.

But we can't afford to not watch the news these days because the devastation could lead anywhere close to home.

We should be prepared and know what to pray for and against. We need you. Someone needs your prayers desperately. God is a proven way maker. He moves mountains (things that harass or irritate you) out of your way. He is bigger than any legal trouble, any case, any battle, any deadly disease, any addiction, mental disorder, depression, generational curses or poverty.

You can overcome anything because Jesus overcame the world. He is bigger than ignorance or a lack of knowledge or education. He's the giver of light and wisdom. The holy spirit will make you smarter than a person with a 5 star education and God can elevate you and put you in powerful positions that humans think you aren't worthy of.

Who cares what they think anyway? You can't compare the supernatural to the average flesh. The average person who is a non-believer cannot fathom having faith and believing in the unbelievable and unseeable things.This is exactly why you can't look at things in the natural realm. You can't accept the way things look in life. You must elevate and look at life from a higher perspective. Unbelievers don't agree you can create the life you want and attract the most beautiful things and people in the spirit realm. But it's true. Surround yourself with people you love and admire that add value, warmth, wisdom and biblical support to your life. That's the power of God on your very being. Some unbelievers have been religiously persuaded to believe there are multiple ways to get to God. That is a myth!

Jesus said to him, "I am the {only} way {to God} and the {real} truth and the {real} life; No one comes to the Father but through me.
(John 14:6 Amp)

That right there, is as plain as it gets. You cannot serve random religions that don't worship God and not acknowledge the truth about Jesus. Not saying you must only and always pray to Jesus, because Jesus is not God. God is God the Father. You most certainly can pray to God too. Jesus is the son of God and he was temporarily God in the physical form. He was his representative speaking on his behalf. He most certainly is the messiah and he will return again. God is the ultimate. You can't let humans create doubt in your mind about who God or Jesus is without studying the word for yourself. You shouldn't then decide to follow some religion or spiritual practice that feels "good" to you and call it God. Do not be a follower and let people cast uncertainty in your mind that there is not a biblical heaven and hell so that you feel comfortable in your sin without the burden of fatal consequences.

That is a myth! Read the word for yourself. Do not think its the same or you're going to reach him your own way. When praying to false Gods your prayers are falling on deaf ears. If you feel in life you're doing well it's no fault of your own but because he is so merciful and he loves you anyway. He's giving you time and mercy to come to him. Even if when we don't love or choose him, that's how awesome he is. Despite our sin, the Father loves us anyway. He doesn't love the sin but he still cares for us greatly. He's hoping we'll come home and we'll choose sacred love over the world.

The word also says whatever you ask in Jesus name shall be given. The power of the name of Jesus is nothing short of miraculous. This world is too dangerous and life is to short to take a gamble. It's a risk to worship satan. And I know some will say I don't worship satan, I love God. I just don't feel I have to live according to his laws. I can love him and do me. Well lets see....

No one can serve two masters; for either he will hate the one and love the other, or he will stand by and be devoted to the one and despise and be against the other. You cannot serve God and mammon (deceitful riches, money, possessions, or whatever is trusted in). (Matthew 6:24, AMP)

Whatever you want to know, its in the word. There should be no confusion but there often is. The world has false teachers and leaders claiming to be lead by God, misleading truth seekers. Indeed there are false prophets out there and we should all be aware. They existed in ancient times and they exist now, teaching things that are not biblical and misleading the congregation. Teaching their personal interpretations and giving holiness a bad reputation. Some are bending and twisting the scriptures to be politically correct and not offend political figures, church members or the media. Others are in the pulpit preaching ME sermons. Those are sermons to bend the word to fit the preachers lifestyle and excuse their own sins.

Thats pure foolishness. If you're at any place of worship where the Rabbi (teacher) is not giving biblical instructions and just talking off the top of their head. Run! For the nearest exit, your life is at stake! Get to the nearest bible in a understandable, truthful translation and seek him. Anyone bringing the word to Gods people should be anointed, lead by the holy spirit and following the decrees themselves.

(Anointing: having the power of God upon you to do something). Leaders should not be hypocrites and teach lies. Church leaders should not just teach positive thinking. Portions of the bible must not be omitted because this is the 21st century or a social media driven society. The law is the law. The commandments and decrees have not been deleted from history or from the bible. We must not change the Sabbath from Saturday the 7th day to Sunday the 1st day because it suits our schedules better. Sunday worship is wonderful but should not be the only day of recognition to visit the temple. Our lives should be scheduled around the Holy day not the other way around. The New Testament does not invalidate the old. The exodus from Egypt did happen and Moses was a real person. It's not just a story book.

For the time is coming when [people] will not tolerate (endure) sound and wholesome instruction, but, having ears itching [for something pleasing and gratifying], they will gather to themselves one teacher after another to a considerable number, chosen to satisfy their own liking and to foster the errors they hold. 4) And will turn aside from hearing the truth and wander off into myths and man-made fictions. 5) As for you, be calm and cool and steady, accept and suffer unflinchingly every hardship, do the work of an evangelist, fully perform all the duties of your ministry. (2 Timothy 4:3-5 Amp)

I recently saw a interview of a mega pastor who I like a lot and he was directly asked if homosexuality was a sin? He did everything under the sun to change the subject, he was literally shaking. He downright refused to answer the question. What's so hard about saying well according to the Bible its a sin.

Done. You're a man of God was that so hard to say. That's like denying God. He was literally sweating and the Holy Spirit immediately revealed to me, he's not lead by the anointing. He's self ordained. Then I remembered he was placed in his position because of a death in his family. Sometimes there's a desire to lead or be popular by any means necessary.

You don't have to manipulate or be ashamed of the truth. It's not okay to attack or hate people who make different choices. If you don't agree with a persons lifestyle, it's not your place to be viscous just to be heard. It's also not okay for people to attack religious or biblical beliefs because you feel it condemns your lifestyle. The bible clearly says what God loves and hates. We have to get to place of compassion and healthy communication but most of all do it in love. Stand firm in what you believe, just make sure you're on a solid foundation of evidence supporting your position. Men and women of God who are lead by his power and who love to bring people to Christ are excited about sharing the word in a loving way.

The truth shall set you free indeed. You can't be concerned with people getting mad, you're just the messenger, you didn't make the rules.

Neither are you enforcing them, you're just sharing what the bible says. It's not like he was out in the streets crucifying and placing open judgements. He was asked a simple question. Is it a sin in the bible? We love to identify and label a multitude of sins as if one is worst or better.

As if that makes any sense.

#SinisSin #GodIsTheOnlyJudge

I must trust God and be bold as a lion and stand on the word, knowing he has my back.

Otherwise it's performance based living, by trying to make things happen on my own, instead of trusting his word. Positive thinking with no biblical basis doesn't get you into the kingdom of heaven. As a man or woman of God you must teach the truth according to the scripture. Nothing else will do. Check this out.

> Beware of false prophets [teachers], who come to you dressed as sheep, [appearing gentle and innocent] but inwardly are ravenous wolves. By their fruits you will recognize them.[That is, by their contrived doctrines and self-focus] Do people pick grapes from thorn bushes, or figs from thistles? Even so, every healthy tree bears good fruit but the unhealthy trees bears bad fruit (Matthew 7:15-17, Amp)

Some may say, how can I decide if my Rabbi or Pastor is legit or i'm at the right ministry. This is why you must know the Lord for yourself. It's astounding how many people don't fact check what they're taught by spiritual leaders. I was raised up in the church but grew spiritually in a Jewish temple. And everything I knew about the Bible and Torah was taught to me, including broken scriptures. Bits and pieces of passages that were taken out of context intentionally and taught. It wasn't until I was an adult and studied the entire Bible that I found the truth and realized I had been misguided my whole life. In fact some of our parents who taught us these mistruths have been misguided for decades and the chain goes back generations.

This is why you must study your scriptures for yourself. It seems to be up to the current generations to shed light to millions globally who are in the dark and unaware of the marvelous works of the Messiah. We must clear up the myths and encourage people to truly engage in Biblical studies and intense prayer in order to wake up. Besides, the only way to become a Miracle Magnet is to know the word by heart. This is why we must be lead spiritually, because our guide is pure and without mistakes.

The holy spirit is more than just a comforter, he's a revealer and a compass. He'll tug at your heart when something's not right or he'll warm your soul with a true revelation. It's such a gift that very few experience because they aren't dedicated to diving into the word and don't devote the time to having a special relationship with the lord. Quickly, you will be enlightened super naturally and see things in the spirit world that others can't see. It will blow your mind and you'll be astonished and overwhelmed but soon you'll feel honored. Revel in his awesomeness and really take in that its honorable to embrace this gift.

The ability to be used as some of the greatest women and men of the bible were, will have you praying for more exposure to scriptures. Lord show me signs and wonders of your goodness. Give me all the gifts of the Holy Spirit and use me in a powerful way. I have seen the most miraculous things in my lifetime. Unexplainable things. Once after fervently praying and studying about the blood of Jesus and about the story of the Passover. I passionately sought God for a supernatural sign and to speak to my heart and show me I wasn't crazy and imagining the dreams I had. Then as clear as the sun was shining I saw a full lambs head in the sky. I gasped in shock and asked the woman standing next to me what did she see in the sky? Without telling her what I saw.

She said "Wow, it looks like a sheep or a lambs head but it's for sure one or the other"! In shock, I said thank you Father, it's now confirmed that you answered my prayer and that it's more than okay to ask him for signs and wonders, because he will. Now you may say there are shapes in the sky all the time. But what are the typical chances that i'd be studying about the Lamb of God that day and then pray for signs and wonders. Walk outside, look up and see a full lambs head. The feeling was astounding to me. I will never forget that day.

I knew God was all powerful but I was new to learning about supernatural revelations. This was the lord confirming that the blood of Jesus is real and the blood of the lamb slain not only represents Christ but was a epic triumph in the history for the Jews. It is to be studied and meditated on constantly to become stronger and wiser daily. Faith is not something that can be stored up and saved for a rainy day. It has to be renewed daily by the hearing and reading of the word. Last year while studying revelations and stories about sea monsters in the bible, I saw Dragon shaped clouds, i've also had prophetic dreams that came true. For example, I had a dream about locusts and I woke up in a sweat like lord, give me revelation, what does that mean. I thought it was kind of creepy at first and I was a bit shaken. I mean who dreams about locust? I hadn't before. Then as clear as day I heard the lord speak to my heart and say, "I will repay you for the years the locust has eaten from your life". I had no clue what it meant? Then I researched the scriptures later that morning during my bible study.

*And I will restore or replace for you the years that the locust has
eaten—the hopping locust, the stripping locust, and the crawling locust,
My great army which I sent among you.(Joel 2:25 Amp)*

I was like ok, thank you lord because the devil has stolen a lot of things from me and I want it back plus more! Shortly after I recreated by business

I received unbelievable increases in an abundance of supplies. Even my adult children were creating thousands of dollars at a time consistently out of nowhere, all at the same time. I received miracles after miracles, and when God moves he moves in a mighty way and when he blesses you, everyone attached to you, especially your household will be blessed.

Remember it's okay to not understand something you feel you hear from God or a dream you may have. The holy spirit will interpret it for you and give you the tools to expound if you ask. Trust and believe living a life dedicated to service to God and winning souls to christ is not boring by any means. There are phenomenal rewards for your obedience and what you give up in the natural is crumbs of nothing compared to what you'll gain spiritually. Satan does not love us, he gives rewards too, because he wants followers and bodies in his army.

It's important to live a life of complete surrender & total dependence on God. Don't straddle the fence or swing on the coat-tails of the prayers of the righteous. Create a deep prayer life for yourself. You'll experience a joy and peace you've never imagined and power that feeds your soul mightily. Trust me it's better than your best dream ever.

Step 4: Stand Firm On Who God Truly Is To You

Side Note: The Bible Is Like A Juicy Novel… You'll Fall Out Your Chair. I Dare You To Indulge.

Fearless As A Raging Lioness

The bible says " Don't be Afraid!" Multiple times.

Do not fear [anything], for I am with you; Do not be afraid, for I am your God. I will strengthen you, be assured I will help you; I will certainly take hold of you with My righteous right hand [a hand of justice, of power, of victory, of salvation]. (Isaiah 41: 10 Amp)

I remember the depiction of Jesus on the boat on the Sea of Galilee with the disciples. As a storm brewed they woke him up frantic in fear shouting "Lord save us, we're going to die!".

Then Jesus got up and rebuked the winds and the sea calmed. They looked in amazement and Jesus said "Why were you afraid? Why were you afraid when I was with you?". This is so powerful to me, it literally just gave me chills, because it's a great question even now. Why are we so afraid when Jesus is with us. You would think, why would they be afraid and they were physically with him. We can't see Jesus here but they did.

In my mind, I'm like, you are literally in the same boat with Jesus and in that moment you were still terrified? They saw him alive and were sitting a few inches away from him and yet still were afraid. They were with him at an Epic time in history when he was outperforming himself in miracles, but yet no trust. I would have been napping right along with Jesus on that boat with no worries had I witnessed such sightings. I'm sure of it, because I witnessed it for myself.

However that goes to show not only the power of fear but the power of unbelief.

The wicked flee when no man pursues them, but the [uncompromisingly] righteous are bold as a lion. (Proverbs 28:1 Amp)

We sometimes are naturally still afraid even though God is with us. Although we can't see his face, we can feel his presence in our lives.

There's no need to be afraid, especially if you practice being in his presence. Study and trust in his word to protect you. God just wants us to believe in him the way he believes in us. Imagine how confident and fearless you'd be, if he was standing right in front of you. Imagine that now, because he is. You may not be able to see him, but surely can feel his presence in the room, in your life and in your body like you can feel a jacket on your back. Sometimes in the spirit realm, I imagine seeing twelve foot Angels standing in the corners of my room. I also see them beside me walking down the street.

I feel such protection and peace and I go about my day unbothered. I truly know they are surely there. When I feel a little anxiety trying to creep up to make me insecure about the future, I thank God for those Angels of protection surrounding me. Who are looking out for me, standing by my side to let the devil know, I have backup. When I pray I slay. I say lord I release the warring angels to go forth and fight battle on my behalf as I rest in you. You must take the dominion and authority that you have in this world.

And God blessed them and said to them, Be fruitful, multiply, and fill the earth, and subdue it [using all its vast resources in the service of God and man]; and have dominion over the fish of the sea, the birds of the air, and over every living creature that moves upon the earth. (Genesis 1:28 Amp)

Now let me be transparently honest here, as far I can recall, I've lived in doubt and fear since I was a very young girl. I lived in constant terror and under traumatic conditions. I understand best that having a brutal childhood, making tough decisions as a minor and being surrounded by unkind adults will trigger self doubt and dream genocide. It will make you question if God is real. Does he love me? Why am I here? Why did he allow this to happen to me? All valid questions we've all asked ourselves.

God doesn't hurt us, the enemy does. However sometimes God may allow things to take place in our lives for the purpose of his glory, or because we have brought things on ourselves.

It all shapes us into who we are today. Truthfully the father doesn't normally bring troubles our way, it's the devil who's number one job is to bring agony into every life on earth. We live in a dangerous and evil world and sometimes bad things happen. If things happen to you beyond your control then it's not your fault and God will avenge you. Although we must take responsibility for the things that have happened within our control. I truly believe nothing will change if there is no responsibility taken. And apologies mean nothing without changed behavior. If we continue to choose the same we'll get the same results. Taking control of that starts with being prayed up and suited for warfare. Fear keeps the anointing from working in your life. Fear only empowers your enemies so remember that the next time you're slipping unconsciously into defeat. It salivates on our doubt like a vicious dog on a raw steak and wants to destroy your anointing and any chances of you being great in any capacity.

Think about this. What would your life look like without fear? What if you did everything you put your hands, mind and heart too. What would the outcome look like? How much would you conquer on a daily basis? How fired up and motivated would you be to carry out task after task? Write all of these questions down and answer them. I'd bet you'd be unstoppable because your confidence in yourself would be strengthened by faith. We've become dependent on fear as a way to protect ourselves from disappointment and hurt. Not allowing ourselves to feel joy and happiness because we're afraid it won't last. That's no way to live and that way of thinking is a setup for failure.

Faith helps you to take a dream out of the Euphoria of an idea and transmit it into the realm of possessions and tangible things. Faith is the connection between God and man. So basically faith is not positive thinking or wishing for the best. It is truly understanding that there is a difference between the physical and spiritual worlds and this world is in a spiritual war. As humans we've had our foot in two worlds from the beginning of time. The human world and the spirit world. Good VS. Evil. If you remember that at all times, you will never be knocked off your feet and you'll win every battle.

Faith is also not the product of logical reasoning but refusing to look and accept things the way they are naturally. It's trusting and believing what the Bible says instead of what you see. It's hoping and believing God for the greatest outcome. Its saying I will trust in the Lord no matter what circumstances I see right now. No matter what man says. No matter what the Judge or doctor says. No matter what my bank account or creditors say. No matter what my parents or family say. No matter what social media says.

The physical world will have you thinking that you are doomed and you might as well go jump off a building because it's over for you. Forget those lies that say you'll never live a quality life and it only gets worse off from here; or blessings don't happen for people like you. All lies from the deep pits of torment. That's what he wants you to think so you are completely distracted from reading books like this. He wants you distracted from regaining your energy and getting your artillery together.

That's when he sneaks up from the back and attacks you in the worst ways. Don't fall for it and fight Back! The Bible is a playbook on how to defeat all your enemies like a ruler. Be like a roaring lioness, since she knows when a woman reigns like a king, she's a Kween. I call it a double throne.

Now faith is the assurance (the confirmation, the title deed) of the things [we] hope for, being the proof of things [we] do not see and the conviction of their reality [faith perceiving as real fact what is not revealed to the senses]. (Hebrews 11:1 Amp)

I disregarded family and friends telling me to accept defeat and don't fight the inevitable. Sounds crazy right? If I had a dollar and listened to everybody who didn't believe in me when they saw me facing an impossible situation. I'd be a Billionairess. You can't listen to haters who don't have the grain of a mustard seed faith in their own life. They're defeated and lack faith and give up when things look tough for themselves. They have no dominion or claim any authority over anything other than being overly religious and going to church weekly.

You can't listen to people who lack a true intimacy and truthful understanding of who the Messiah really is. Being religious counts for nothing but being super judgemental. Praying and going to church consistently is not enough to get you into the kingdom. Anyone who believes that just doesn't know or know the scriptures. You can tell the people who have unwavering faith and know the Miracles and power it creates. You can hear in the way they talk everyday.

Remember the scriptures about knowing them by their fruits because those leaders will stand by you in faith and biblically advise you. If Jesus could turn water into wine and heal the lame and give sight to the blind. Why can't he fix your troubles? I've obtained mountains of Miraculous wins this way, and had avalanches of blessings fall in my lap. All because i've refused to die in defeat. All because i'm mastering the power of faith. I study the word daily and I listen to teachings daily. I feed my innerman and I pray in the spirit and most of all, I worship in spirit and truth. This will remind you, God dispatches legions of Angels at your side everyday.

He loves you and wants you to live a good, abundant life. Satan counts on you getting weak with uncertainty and looking at the roadblocks. He wants so much to be like God but he's not.

His power is limited. You only energize his power when you fall for his tricks of doubt and give him him a body to inhabit. Don't entertain his foolishness and keep your foot on his neck so he doesn't get his on yours. He flees at the sight of a faith-filled person and he trembles at the very name of Jesus. You want to get the devil off your back? Decree it! Satan, the blood of Jesus is against you! There is only one God.

That men may know from the east and the rising of the sun and from the west and the setting of the sun that there is no God besides Me. I am the Lord, and no one else [is He].
(Isaiah 45:6 Amp.)

You must stay in his presence and study these scriptures and you'll see your fear start to fall away. Fear is a spirit designed to intimidate you and turn you away from your dreams and goals. It's a scare tactic to back you into silence, intimidation and submission. Fear wants you to fold like a pretzel and make you cower like a kitten in a corner. Fear wants you to deny christ, deny your gifts and deny your very power on this planet. It wants you to wake up and forget the dream you just had. Find your power in Christ because with God for you, who in the world can be against you. You are a mighty lion so your faith must be extremely aggressive. The same way your life is under attack and the enemy goes after you job, families etc. Be vigilant and stern with your defense.

For God did not give us a spirit of timidity (of cowardice, of craven and cringing and fawning fear), but [He has given us a spirit] of power and of love and of calm and well-balanced mind and discipline and self-control. (2 Timothy 1: 7, Amp.)

Step 5: Never Concern Yourself With What Sheeps Think, You're A Lion

Side Note: Fight To Win, Not To Get Whipped

The Battle Over Your Mind

"Knowing The Power Of Her Mind,
She Decided To Think Better"
AJ Williams

Thoughts are like a video screen playing on the imaging of your mind and if you're not careful, you could create undesirable things. We can also shift unwanted events. We determine the life we want through visual thoughts and faith. Your mind is a very powerful entity and a changed mind is even more effective. Over the years I've learned that once your mindset changes everything around you will change as well. You must be unreasonable and not make any excuses as to why you can't get things done or live a great life. There was always a reason why I couldn't do something and I was great at saying i'll do it tomorrow, next month or next year. Don't settle for safe or any other excuses that you don't have the time. If you could see the future and what you're missing, you would make the time.

If there's something you want bad enough you will make it happen. Remember life seems like forever but it really isn't. We're only here for a short time and there's joy and happiness beyond your past mistakes and struggles. Now is the time while your mind is the sharpest because its receptive and open to new ideas or you wouldn't be reading this book. Train your mind to think what you want by visualizing all the wonderful things you'd like to do and have.

Brainstorm various business ideas and imagine what it would be like to experience those amazing accomplishments. Entertain the idea of you being a super bad (meaning good), bossed up traveling the world, making life better everywhere you go type of woman. A shifting the atmosphere cause you're here type of woman. A people get blessed, saved and healed because you're in the building type of woman. That's a powerful action point and exactly the lifestyle i've always desired to lead. The anointing will give you success in all areas of your life. The reason successful people are successful because they don't ever entertain the idea of failure. No matter if its a short term possibility, they stay laser focused on what they actually want to attract and that's what they get. Failure is not an option. If you don't know where to start ask God for creative money making ideas and he'll give you direct strategies and never give you a vision without provision. He won't just give you a cute idea without providing you with direct resources or opening doors. If he did, it would make him a liar and he can't do that. It's impossible for God to lie.

That's just who he is and what he does. He operates in the unknown and does the impossible. It's why he's so amazing and it doesn't matter who or what you are. Don't let that factor into you not at least formulating a written plan. What I normally do since being a teen, is get a pen and a really cute notebook, sit down and think about what it is that i'd absolutely love to do. I'd write all my dreams out and everything I wanted. Then jot down my strengths and what i'm not really good at as well. The next step is to figure out what's in your ability to do right now, today. There's always a step you could take in the present moment. Never put off tomorrow what you could do today so just take it one step at a time. Don't overwhelm yourself or your mind by overloading on minor details. Don't think to far down the road. That's the biggest distraction ever and we get away from ourselves and then get discouraged.

Just stay present in the joy of seeing what's possible and giving yourself credit for moving forward and pushing through adversity. Look at me for example, i've been a writer since I was a kid. I wrote my first worship song at 5 years old and since written thousands of poems, scripts, and songs but it's taken over 10 years to write this book. I've started and stopped over the years. I've written a chapter or two and walked away for years. I allowed fearful thoughts of failure to consume my mind and it scared me away from my own destiny temporarily. Imagine that. Being scared away from something that' apart of your DNA. It would be tragic to be scared away from doing something God has called you to do. Especially something that could alter lives in a great way. Honestly once I made up my mind and sat down and started writing, the words flowed through my soul like water. It was like I couldn't stop myself and my hands were being controlled by someone else. I kept studying and after meditating, I was glued to my chair and God would give me the content chapter after chapter. I couldn't walk away from my laptop as God was feeding my spirit, I prayed for anointed wisdom for this book. I would stay up all night praying and seeking him with excitement into the next day still writing all fired up.

The most amazing part, is he was blessing me through it all. Re-affirming himself to me as I reread my own words. This book is for the people but it's also for myself. I read this book often to hear from the Lord and stay on track. I recite these very prayers. All because I made up my mind and took action and trusted him to do the rest. Now that its finally complete, it's opened up so many doors and opportunities for me to share the love of christ with thousands of people. I wish i'd done this years ago, but at the same time everything is about timing. Maybe my wisdom wouldn't be developed for this to be a successful guide. Maybe I answered the call at just the right time after I went through the most meaningful but devastating storms.

Storms that shaped me into the woman that I've become today. Storms with the kind of harsh whirlwinds that propelled me into my destiny and made me roar the name of God. Sometimes to get a real breakthrough you have to get to a place of desperation in your life for things to truly change. You have to be totally over done with what you've been dealing with and come to the throne of grace with a humble open heart. It will be a total surrender of all that you are for the transformation and healing to really begin.

I am however grateful for my experiences and maturity which makes every new endeavor more amazing and it's given me the confidence to move forward and complete other things in my life that needed attention and healing. It's bringing healing to my life as I'm writing these very words, because i'm reminded constantly of how he saved me and didn't give up on me. He waited for me because he saw something in me that I didn't see in myself. I too was in the world in sin, taking risk and setting myself up for epic fails. I realized he loves me more than anyone on this earth could ever love me. God is so reliable to hold your hand while guiding you into your calling so pray and ask to see yourself the way he does.

He treasures you and you're beautiful and lovely in his eyes. The fact remains, if we only saw ourselves the way the bible says God sees us and loves us, we wouldn't be so quick to discredit ourselves. We wouldn't believe what haters say about us. It's important for women to stay in control of our mental capacity when we get involved in relationships. Men think more logically than we do on matters of the heart.

Although we think more logically than they do normally in other areas. The matters of the heart are most important because allowing yourself to release your inhibitions can be very harmful.

> *Keep and guard your heart with all vigilance and above all that you guard, for out of it flow the springs of life. (Proverbs 4:23 Amp)*

When we allow ourselves to lose restraints emotionally it can cloud judgements. Love without consciousness becomes need, dependency and control and it puts some of us in a position of giving our power away. That's why I really understand the concept of act like a lady but think like a guy. They say that because we tend to think and lead with our hearts and emotions, while men think logical mostly. That's why it's so easy for some men to call a woman crazy when she's really not. It's a easy cop-out because they know we're being emotional and thinking with our hearts not our minds. It's easier for them to say that instead of taking responsibility for adding stress, heartache or putting us through the cycle of betraying commitments.

They call women crazy and poke fun to draw the attention away from their contribution to the heightened intensity of the situation. We all know that's a revolving door or a constant ride on the merry go round. Girl get off that ride, because the trick is to literally drive you crazy. Mental wellness is imperative to leading a successful life in this world and in Christ. For example someone who's overly emotional and broken hearted may not make the best choices concerning intelligent matters. I know the decisions i've made when I was clear and sober minded verses when I was hurt and afraid are completely different. You have to balance logic and emotions since emotional intelligence leads to success in all areas. It's never wise to make a decision when your angry, unless you're making the decision to not be angry and get over it. There are no excuses, only choices, and sometimes the choices that we're left with are not great options.

That is when you create new options. Now don't get me wrong, we all know that some men can be very emotional as well. It's not just us.

However it's a very rare breed of men who act feminine and overly emotional and irrational. Always wanting to have the last word, purposely pushing your buttons instead of defusing the situation as well as being moody and petty. Some don't know how to push the off button for the sake of peace. That's why we must stay in control because two angry and uncontrollable adults is a recipe for disaster.

Keep your head on straight, chin up and brain right. Thank God he's a mind regulator, he'll get you together very well and have you sitting pretty, blessed and in control. It's a very good practice to meditate on the word because it'll regulate your life and give you peace. Our father also controls our moods and can balance the whole ecosystem so keeping your mental health happy is key. If that stays on point then the truth about what's available to you and what you're entitled to can continue to be revealed and increase your faith. You decide what thoughts you think and what you take captive and dispose of.

[In as much as we] refute arguments and theories and reasonings and every proud and lofty thing that sets itself up against the [true] knowledge of God; and we lead every thought and purpose away captive into the obedience of Christ (the Messiah, the Anointed One).
(2 Corinthians 10:5 Amp)

The mind is the devils gateway and doorway into our souls. That's how he enters your body so you must guard your thoughts and fiercely protect what you meditate on. The most potent form of energy is your thoughts since they become things, actions and words. Your mind can be programmed to think and attract what you want. You can also program your mind to not focus on what you don't want. So shut those thoughts down by feeding your brain and heart the word of God daily. Your psyche could easily be compared to a computer since it could download a virus that produces defective choices. I have seen the face of mental illness and what it can do to a person who can't seem to connect and hear the voice of God.

All because they're consumed with thoughts, pain and emotions. I've witnessed folks go off the deep end with their emotions and not be able to pump the brakes for the sake of not damaging their own lives. Normally we consider the mentally ill to be a person walking down the street talking to themselves. It's assumed that they have been diagnosed with a disorder. The reality is there's a large population who suffer from various mental conditions that are regular people. A crisis or devastating trauma can be overwhelming. This can trigger conditions in the brain that lead to poor decision making or depression.

When your mind is broken and can't seem to function right it's a stronghold. Sin starts in the mind first and then dominates the spirit and body. Strongholds are a mental block of materialism, secularism, sexism, sensationalism, worry, guilt, fear and lust. Strongholds are set up to go against the word of God. The wonderful thing is that you don't have to believe everything you think. The bible says that satan is the father of lies. He loves to suggest lies and untrue thoughts and if your not strong enough mentally, you'll fall for it every time.

You are of your father, the devil, and it is your will to practice the lusts and
gratify the desires [which are characteristic] of your father. He was a murderer
from the beginning and does not stand in the truth, because there is no truth in
him. When he speaks a falsehood, he speaks what is natural to him, for he is a liar
[himself] and the father of lies and of all that is false. (John 8:44. Amp.)

Just because something pops in your head doesn't mean its real or will come to pass. You can choose to replace those thoughts with thoughts of blessings and good things and focus on that. Meditate until it becomes a daily habit and positive thinking becomes a way of life for you. The bible also speaks of even a royal King having a troubled mind.

Therefore the mind of the king of Syria was greatly troubled by
this thing. He called his servants and said, Will you show me who
of us is for the king of Israel? (2 Kings 6:11 Amp)

Your mental monologue cannot contain self-defeating psycho babble or you'll create that exact life that terrifies you the most. A spirit of heaviness most often accompanies those self-defeating conceptions that plague us. This translates into the physical. Most often it's usually not clinical depression but mental oppression brought on by a spiritual battle.

These are spiritual attacks on your mind, and the enemy is warring God for our entire lives. Once and if he wins, he inhabits your body because you're no longer in control. You're just a host. It's like watching a horror movie when a evil spirit or alien takes over a humans body.

They no longer have control over their will and that's the way the enemy works in this world. It's my reason for being merciful towards certain people who haven't been delivered yet. I have spiritual understanding that it's not the person you love and care for, but rather the spirit they are controlled by making them behave that way. As for myself, when I look back over my life and look at my past and things i've done that i'm not proud of. I think Wow, that wasn't me at all. I was out of my mind and irrational, clearly checked out to lunch. There's no way in a million years I would have done or allowed certain things; had I been free and clear minded. I even remember doings that I promised myself I wouldn't, next thing you know I find myself in the process of doing just that. I'm like how did this happen? I don't remember starting, so I could remind myself not to do this. It's like an out of body experience where it isn't realized until you're in the action. Have you ever told yourself I'm not doing this anymore? Only to find yourself doing it again. And again. That's corruption of the highest level. The enemy knows how to make things appealing and he can show you wonders and signs as well, so be aware. That relates to that feeling of being stuck or feeling paralyzed by fear. It's also similar to addiction. That's why some addicts can cold turkey stop and be delivered on the spot and others battle and toil helplessly.

Addiction affects the mind, which effects the body, which then affects your actions. Once a persons brain is controlled, then their will is gone and the body follows. From that point they need assistance to regain control of their life with spiritual and mental rehabilitation.

Humanity should be compassionate and non judgmental towards the less fortunate because they need our help. Their lives could be saved if they're minds are renewed.

Do not be conformed to this world (this age), [fashioned after and adapted to its external, superficial customs], but be transformed (changed) by the [entire] renewal of your mind [by its new ideals and its new attitude], so that you may prove [for yourselves] what is the good and acceptable and perfect will of God, even the thing which is good and acceptable and perfect [in His sight for you]. (Romans 12:2 Amp.)

Step 6: Ask The Lord To Direct And Guard Your Mind

Side Note: Discipline Is A Trait Of A Powerful Woman.

How To Be A Miracle Magnet

There's a miracle in your mouth but it can't be activated spiritually without speaking it. It must be declared and released in the spirit world or it's illegal in the natural realm. It's incredible to realize there are bona fide miracles with your name on it out there, just floating through time and space not being called into your reality. You must breathe life into your dreams through your words. Speak your favorite scriptures into existence. The bible says there is power in the tongue and in the name of Jesus.

> *Death and life are in the power of the tongue, and they who indulge in it*
> *shall eat the fruit of it [for death or life]. (Proverbs 18:21 AMP.)*

Decree I'm close to favor and promotion and i'm closer than i've ever been. My thoughts are on good things and miracles overtake my life. And i'm living in the overflow of abundance. Just because you don't see it at the moment doesn't mean that God isn't working on your behalf.

Declare that I walk in divine favor and protection and the anointing of God is upon me in all that I do with my hands. My family is blessed and I have wealth and financial increase to live a premium life. My finances bless the kingdom of God and my family. I have preferred treatment everywhere I go. Keep seeking the Lord, speaking his truths and he will work wonders on your behalf. Once you understand this phenomenal power it's really a game changer.

I've literally turned the worse situations in my life around by faith and speaking life. I've seen numerous Miracles, to the point that I've had to create a note called "Won't he Do It". It's a catalog of miraculous blessings I've received.

Just so I wouldn't forget and I can always refer back to it and replenish my spirit. Especially when I feel my faith is being tested. I've seen God remove obstacles and i've prayed people away from me. I even asked God to reveal phony friends and if a man was being unfaithful to me. And He did just that. However i'm human so sometimes I wasn't prepared for the answers.

So i've learned to be careful and very strategic about what I pray for because it takes maturity to handle what he reveals. Prayer is a powerful weapon to be utilized to accumulate results. I prayed for all the spiritual gifts and for my spirit of discernment to be intensified. He granted that too and it's something I wasn't prepared for after I prayed about it. It's crucial to understand the powers can't be played around with and must be properly handled.

At a young age I was blessed with the gift of discernment and I felt like it was a gift and a curse. I felt this way because I couldn't handle that it allowed me to see spiritual things I didn't understand and that I didn't want to see. It revealed secret things about people I didn't want to know but couldn't ignore. You know that feeling of seeing a person a certain way and once something is exposed about them, you can't just forget it. It's like I can't just un-know this information. Just like you can't unsay something hurtful to a person. After making so many bad choices, I prayed for supernatural discernment and it gave me a better judgement system.

This leads to making rewarding choices that translates into an awesome life. Our father wants us living the good life and in good health. The world is not supposed to be living better than the people of God. Although it may appear that way in terms of materialism, but those are only temporal earthly things with no heavenly treasures. It doesn't last and it's only a facade. Always remember that everything that seems impressive is not a blessing. The devil blesses his people too and he dangles things and possessions in our faces to lure us on his side. It's important to recognize that Gods people are living very well. Not just Rabbis, Pastors and Evangelist but also people in other fields that love the lord.

Individuals with great character, high powered jobs and entrepreneurs running their business the kingdom way. He blesses housewives, the unemployed and the broken hearted. He can increase anyone from any walk of life. You just need to meet and fellowship with him. It's such a myth that religious people are called to be poor and that money is evil. That's untrue. You shouldn't love money but rather value each other and holiness. There's a changing of the guards shifting the atmosphere. The world has been controlling the money, possessions and the land and now the people of God are taking the reclaim with Dominion and Authority. We are taking back all the blessings we allowed to be stolen from us. It's our birthright according to the word.

Check this out.

And that you may live long in the land which the Lord swore to your fathers to give to them and to their descendants, a land flowing with milk and honey. (Deuteronomy 11:9, Amp)

There's an abundance of blessings, miracles and wealth flowing through out congregations worldwide. It's because people are finally being taught the infallible word that says we're in a covenant with God. The blessings of this agreement entitles you to what God says you can have according to the Abrahamic covenant. A covenant of favor, wisdom, responsibilities and blessings. The blessings of Abraham are extravagant and abundant. It mentions nothing about constant toiling, struggling to pay bills and being poor for the rest of your life.

And I will make of you a great nation, and I will bless you [with abundant increase of favors] and make your name famous and distinguished, and you will be a blessing [dispensing good to others]. (Genesis 12:2 Amp)

Wow!!! Who doesn't want this? Now there's also the Mosaic Covenant Renewal in Exodus with Moses and the Ten commandments. God then again reiterates the covenant in Deuteronomy. He keeps renewing it so it must be highly significant. How can it not be? To hear new age observances say Oh because of grace we are covered but somehow excused from not honoring the covenant. Um...Where? That would be a humongous mistake. Fatal in fact.

Where does God excuse anyone from not following the decrees and commandments? That's the religious, false prophet man made teaching that will make followers lose their inheritance into the kingdom. We are saved by grace but its not permission to do as we please.

> *Now therefore, if you will obey My voice in truth and keep My covenant,*
> *then you shall be My own peculiar possession and treasure from among and*
> *above all peoples; for all the earth is Mine. (Exodus 19:5 Amp)*

There are to many doctrines and ideologies out there convincing people to turn away from following the word. Obedience not perfection is a must.

> *For just as by one man's disobedience (failing to hear, heedlessness,*
> *and carelessness) the many were constituted sinners, so by one Man's*
> *obedience the many will be constituted righteous (made acceptable to God,*
> *brought into right standing with Him). (Romans 5:19 Amp)*

Yes his grace redeems us but obedience to his word obligates us to comply.

> *And God is able to make all grace (every favor and earthly blessing) come to you in*
> *abundance, so that you may always and under all circumstances and whatever the*
> *need be self-sufficient [possessing enough to require no aid or support and furnished*
> *in abundance for every good work and charitable donation].(2 Corin. 9:8 Amp)*

Yes! I need all of that. Sign me up! But please be advised there's also consequences of disobedience to Gods covenants. Be advised that there are curses as well.

Carefully read. **Deuteronomy. 28:15-68** He's saying you, your children and everything you do will be cursed and suffering. He will cause your enemies to defeat you and so forth.

Now have you ever felt like your enemies were defeating you. Have you felt defeated in most areas of your life but you still love the lord and go to church? You wonder what are you doing wrong or what are you not doing right? It's impossible to constantly struggle and be defeated by your enemies if you're obedient. If you fast, pray, give and exercise your faith without doubt, there will be breakthroughs.

You will have the victory in most areas of your life. It's impossible to fail or God would be a liar and that he's not. So with that being said, I ask you again, what are you doing if you are not winning in some capacity in life. It's never to late for him to turn your life in a complete and more favorable direction. Now I know both sides of the coin and believe me it's very true.

It's better to be in the will of God or nothing you have is safe. Choose everlasting life and choose to stand and follow christ into an abundance of Miracles. Remind yourself that you're significant and can be used in mighty ways. Your testimony could be the very thing that saves lives and draw in the broken-hearted and hurting.

Don't ever think he can't use you. Don't you remember the times you've been hurting, where a kind word or hearing someones story could have made all the difference to you. If you study the bible you'll find Gods most profitable and anointed disciples were murderers, liars, fornicators, prisoners and adulterers; all people who God cleaned up. He washed their sins away into the sea of forgetfulness. He transformed their lives and says once you repent, i'll forgive and he did forget, as if it never happened. What human being is that loving or forgiving? No one. He doesn't pick up the phone calling friends and family gossiping about your latest downfall.

God doesn't hold grudges and constantly remind you of your setbacks. He doesn't manipulate and sabotage your future by planting seeds of doubt in your head. He takes you by the hand and says come walk with me, I will give you rest. Just relax and let me do it for you. We stress and work so hard trying to do things in our own strength. Not realizing some things are just out of our control. Let go and let God. You don't have to fight your own battles. You couldn't win them anyway in the flesh. We are no match for evil in these bodies. We must be fitly clothed in the full armor of God and standing in formation, allowing him to lead the way. Not the other way around. He doesn't need our help, we need his.

Behold, all they who are enraged and inflamed against you shall be put to shame and confounded; they who strive against you shall be as nothing and shall perish.12) You shall seek those who contend with you but shall not find them; they who war against you shall be as nothing, as nothing at all. 13) For I the Lord your God hold your right hand; I am the Lord, Who says to you, Fear not; I will help you! (Isaiah 41:11-13, Amp)

This scripture gives me chills. Gods word is truly mighty like a two edged sword. What can you say but Ok Lord. He'll do this for me and you. He's done it for millions of people. If God can take somebody like me, with my childhood, blemished and imperfect past and make me successful. He can do the same for you. Look at the Apostle Paul, he was trying his best to assassinate anyone who professed to love the Lord, until he experienced christ for himself.

Paul became one of Gods greatest and most historic disciples. He was a murderer, a liar and very judgmental and self-righteous. I myself made so many mistakes but he allows me to serve in ministry, teach and has anointed me to help people process who he is. He will use your bad times and turn them into stepping stones for others less fortunate. You must be confident in who you are now and who God is calling you to be. Step out on faith and leave all doubt behind. He will allow you to atone your sins and he'll redeem you. Confidence is the key to activating your faith and standing firm in it. Let go of those past burdens and mistakes.

Did you know bad memories are burdens weighing you down? Rebuke those terroristic thoughts and release your inhibitions. Oh yes, he will terrorize your psyche if you let him. Block negativity. You know those thoughts that make you doubt yourself or a divine idea, you know God gave you. This is where your awareness must be proactive. Now you see the efficacy of being God-conscious. Program yourself for greatness and think about what you want. All it takes is a simple shift in perception. Focus on the blessings and miracles you need.

Focus on what you want, not what you fear the most. You'll attract whatever your mind meditates on. This is not only a universal fact but biblical as well.

> *[In as much as we] refute arguments and theories and reasonings and every*
> *proud and lofty thing that sets itself up against the [true] knowledge of God;*
> *and we lead every thought and purpose away captive into the obedience of*
> *Christ (the Messiah, the Anointed One). (2 Corinthians 10:5, Amp)*

God choosing to save me and not let me die in sin is so precious to me. There's no greater love of redemption and atonement. Nobody was deeper in sin in my eyes. Life was very hard for me growing up. I was physically assaulted and abused on a daily basis since being a young child but I survived. There were many dark times in life when I felt agony. I felt useless because I was unloved and mistreated growing up. I was never told I was loved by anyone in my household other than distant relatives occasionally when I saw them. Some of my darkest hours and most heartfelt anguish were at the hands of someone I loved and trusted dearly. Since then I found Gods love and that has quenched a thirst so deep, that no man can love me enough to replace it. It's incomparable. I don't hold on to anything from the past and I don't allow it to affect my future any more.

God held on to me, he didn't give up on me when everyone else did, even when I wanted to give up on myself. When I didn't believe there was any hope and settled for less than my worth. I fell into a black hole and I mean actually fell out. Literally. Death tried to take me more than once in my lifetime. I've had stray bullets fly past me as a teenager and kill someone walking in front of me and God spared my life. I was innocently walking home from school and walked right through a shoot out. I once narrowly escaped a head-on car collision and later blacked out on concrete floor. I was living but was unconscious. Not really checked in and present the way I needed to be. I didn't see the things that were happening right under my nose and wasn't being accountable for my own actions. If you're not careful, you'll answer the knock at the door and let the inferno in.

Can you imagine being unaware you're sleeping with the enemy until your life is blazing and torched? That's like a secret assassin in your home. Now that's scary. I've learned that extending the hand of constant forgiveness to a repeat offender does more harm than good.

There will be many times when you must show up for yourself firmly and walk away. Your intelligence and emotional discipline will serve you very well. Stay woke and be present and in the moment at all times. Keep your senses sharp and be sensitive to every single person you come in contact with.

Be well balanced (temperate, sober of mind), be vigilant and cautious at all times;
for that enemy of yours, the devil, roams around like a lion roaring [in fierce
hunger], seeking someone to seize upon and devour. (1 Peter 5:8,Amp)

There are so many things we could avoid by focusing on God and staying prayed up and sober. You don't have time to get high or have a glass of wine every night or go days without bible study. You must build your strength and release those charging Angels to do battle for your life. To create victories and miracles in your life, you must know who you're dealing with. Just because you're not dealing with a big test right now, doesn't mean a storm isn't brewing. Be ready. Pray specific battle prayers daily and stay woke.

Know all his characteristics. He's a cunning liar, resourceful, sneaky, diabolical and loves to stir the pot. He'll attack your family, friends, children, job, home and your business. Most important he'll attack your mind and body. He pulls no punches so we shouldn't either. Let me share this testimony. I was sinking in agony and complete despair and dealing with one crisis after the other. One cold winter night in New York everything at home seemed normal. As usual I was silently obsessing and agonizing over my storms. I just got a new job at this big marketing firm in Midtown so I thought my luck was about to change. But it didn't. Ofcourse not, because there's no such thing as luck and I shouldn't have been thinking like that anyway. Especially as a believer. We don't believe in luck.

There's only good fortune, favor, miracles and blessings. No luck. Do you see my state of mind already? I let life cloud my judgement to the point that my praise and my prayers were foggy. I wasn't exercising my faith the way I should have. I had some faith but that was canceled out when doubt crept in. **Lesson learned:** You can't have faith and doubt at the same time because one cancels the other. If you say you believe and have faith, then that's all there is. There's no room for doubt or you cancel what you're believing God for. I was reading scriptures but I wasn't meditating on the word. I was watching sermons but only while I was distracted doing something else, so it didn't resonate.

I missed every workout session I had so there was no buffer to release tension. There was no troubleshooter to moderate the collision I was headed for. I was on autopilot with no brakes and no self-care. I was moving 100 miles an hour and not taking a moment to let my insight and intellect catch up to me physically. This is a bad headspace to be in because this is when it gets dangerous. This is the time in your life when you should be the most calm and sensitive to the holy spirit. When you're standing in turbulence, is when you should be still and say Lord. Whats my next move? I'm feeling defeated and i'm unsure about what to do. I can't trust anyone in my life and I don't even trust myself. I'm overwhelmed by my emotions. Speak to my heart and allow the holy spirit to show me the way. In fact this is one of those times where it's ok to ask for signs and wonders.

Here goes: It's after midnight but I headed out into a snow storm to run an errand. (As i just typed this previous line, i'm thinking to myself, really!) Ok. You headed out into a snow storm to run an errand after midnight? You're thinking what? I know you didn't, but I did, so back to the story. I got into the elevator heading out in 20 degrees weather and highly irritated and frantic. As soon as the doors closed, I immediately felt a dark cloud of haze come over me and my body getting heavy. I'm light-headed, my vision blurred. I feel sleepy…that's all I remember. Until I came too, face down on the concrete floor in a small puddle of my own blood & sweat. My head was split above my eye to the white flesh.

My body was numb and I couldn't feel a thing. How long had I been unconscious? 2, 10, 15 minutes? I'll never know. I was stuck lying in the doorway of the elevator. For those few minutes I was actually blind and paralyzed. I could not move or even shift my pinky finger. I couldn't lift my eyelids. I could not talk. I could not see nor cry. I could only float in another world that was blurry but euphoric. I remember my body felt light as if my spirit was lifting itself up.

These were the longest terrifying moments of my life. I knew I was half body in and half body out of the elevator because I could hear the doors retracting back and forth on my waist. I wanted to move but I was trapped inside my mind. All I could think to do was call on God!

Lord please come to my rescue. It's late so there's no traffic in the lobby of the building. Give me strength. I know your able. I'll change my life and I'll never take my salvation lightly again. I thought about my children being alone in this world. As I lay still and unable to move for a few more minutes, my vision started to slowly clear. I was able to slightly lift my head enough to see a woman come into the lobby, towards me to catch the elevator. She saw me and turned around and decided take the stairs.

Wow right? I know. She couldn't be bothered to help me, but it's ok. Let's give God all the glory he deserves. Now i'm slowly feeling my body and i've got just enough strength to stand. I'm so weak and I can feel myself drifting back in unconsciousness but i'm fighting to keep my eyes open. I'm constantly saying, Lord keep me awake. I decided i'll just stumble outside into the snow, the fresh air will clear me up. Of course that's what I need, fresh air. For some reason people always seem to think that fresh air and water is a great cure for everything. Yea that wasn't a bright idea but you know I'm not thinking clearly anyway. I hear a voice that says don't do that. So I listened. I thrust my body back into the elevator but I couldn't lift my arm to push the button. I waited a few more seconds barely able to lift a finger to press the correct buttons. So I pressed random floors, hoping it would take me to my destination, the 9th floor.

This made me even more anxious because I feel my eyes get heavy and they're closing. I'm slipping backing into unconsciousness and i'm thinking i'm not going to make all these stops. It stopped 3 or 4 times before I actually made it back to my exit. That's all I remember again... until the neighbor across from me found me knocked out lying in the hallway. I could hear him as if I was under water. Mam are you ok? Do you need help? How about that, I passed out again and hit my head on the concrete a second time. Lord Thank you for saving my life a second time tonight. (Miracle 2) I finally made it to safety where the ambulance was called and rushed me to the hospital.

I received medication and stitches. The EMT said mam, had you went outside, you would have died hitting the pavement or by falling on the sharp metal gates outside the front door. Thank You God for sparing me, it could have been so much worse than loss of memory and stitches. Imagine just blacking out in the snow and not being able to break your fall anywhere. Days later, I developed vertigo, my surroundings were dizzy and in motion. It was all bad for a while. Doctors confirmed it was overwhelming anxiety and stress along with not eating regularly. So now I have to deal with this on top of the drama that stressed me to this point. I took one day off and now have to return to work wearing this wrapped head bandage looking like a coma patient.

This occurred at a time in my life when I was uncontrollably crying everyday and night. I literally ate my tears for breakfast and dinner. I was living in utter anguish. I really empathize with people who suffer from all forms of depression and mental illnesses because when the enemy has a lock on your thoughts. It can be mentally lethal when your spirit creates war with your body. I thank God so much for saving me 3 times in one night because weeks prior, elevators were crushing people to death in other buildings. So that could have been tragic as well, but to top it off, I found out I was pregnant a month later. So not only do I thank the father for sparing my life but he saved two lives that night. I could have also had a miscarriage.

As I lay in the ER waiting on my CT scan I remember thinking if I could recall what that unhelpful woman in the lobby looked like. I'd give her a piece of my mind. I imagined myself running into her somewhere in the building one day and saying, what kind of woman are you?

What kind of human would leave another human in that predicament? I could have died! However that will never happen, because I never saw her face, only a female shadow. The truth is, God may have allowed that so he could get the glory when I called his name. He wanted to save me, not some stranger. She did what strangers do. Act strange. Thats between her and God now. I'm just glad to be alive and well.

I'm more consumed with how fearless I am now and how I'm living life to the fullest. This has majorly impacted my destiny. It has influenced me to remove all toxicity, and cut people loose that I love without flinching. It caused me to weigh the value of loved ones based on the value I felt they saw in me. To be insensitive to me at a time like that and cause me unnecessary stress and tears when you saw me suffering.

That's ruthless. We all deserve to be surrounded by compassionate, loving and genuine people that breed harmony. It's like a close friend helping you during a terrible crisis when you're a wreck emotionally. She softly says I got your back girl, i' ll keep your confidence. Meanwhile she's on the bullhorn everyday telling anyone who will listen that she helped you out.

Taking ringside seat side notes and plotting at the same time.

> *Thus, whenever you give to the poor, do not blow a trumpet before you,*
> *as the hypocrites in the synagogues and in the streets like to do, that they*
> *may be recognized and honored and praised by men. Truly I tell you,*
> *they have their reward in full already.(Matthew 6:2 Amp)*

To add insult to injury she's revealing your secrets and most private conversations. Taking advantage of privileged info and using it to her advantage. That kind of help is like a backhanded slap and compliment. Fake friends operate in a type of sorcery to me. If someone who claims to love you and says they have your best interest at heart but behind your back they're doing everything to destroy you. Thats sorcery. You're trying to trick me. You want me to think you're for me {one thing} but behind my back is something else. It reminds me of the snow white witch with the poisonous apple. You're offering fruit, something that looks healthy and good for me but in actuality its harmful. God is not the author of confusion and he doesn't send help like that.

He wants you delivered and restored so he can use you for greater works. It's sad but the enemy will use anybody to hurt you. Specifically those that have a special place in your heart because they have the access. Remove people in your life who upset you and sow discord. You'll be relieved to not question the motives behind why others help you. God will send good reliable people to uplift you. He will open doors and create windows where there was a wall.

Don't ever doubt him. He wants to give us immeasurable favor and victory in all areas. Now I wake up expecting daily miracles. I see them in the lives of my children as well.

Miracles can occur in the form of physical, mental and spiritual healings. Things that happen that you know couldn't have normally happened. When you know, humans couldn't have possibly did this and events occur like heavenly interventions. It's Gods work and it's exceptional when prayers are being answered.

And Jesus increased in wisdom (in broad and full understanding) and in stature and years, and in favor with God and man..(Luke 2:52, Amp)

Step 7: Believe In The Power Of Miracles And Watch Them Appear

Side Note: Don't Let Anyone Make You Feel Unworthy Of Gods Best.

The Power Of Fasting

Fasting is not just going without food or starving. It's refraining from food for spiritual purpose and miracles gains. It's to hear a clear word from the lord in which direction to take in your life. Fasting, praying and trusting God at the same time creates a influential and intimate relationship with the creator. It keeps you sensitive to his spirit and prepares you for a new anointing. Do you need immediate breakthroughs in your life? Do you need miracles and healing? Would you like to feel Gods presence in the deepest way possible? Do you want a deep connection to him? Well this is it. This is like pushing the acceleration button on seeing the manifestation of God over everything you're dealing with. This is an intimate way of communicating with our father.

It's also a great way to establish discipline in your life. If you can't get the victory over your appetite or desires for food, how can you get the victory over spiritual influences? How can you manifest any authority in your life if you're controlled by certain cravings of your favorite foods.

Whatever your vices are or issues that you're struggling with, you can triumph over it. You don't ever have to accept defeat because it's not over until God says it's over. King David was such a worshipper and more than anything he had such a desire to know God on a deeper level. His desire to worship him was greater than his cravings for food as he yearned for the Fathers love and approval. He danced and leaped with joy, unconcerned for the whispers of onlookers. He was excited about the works. I live to feel his hand on me because that kind of peace is indescribable and satisfying. From the moment I witnessed a supernatural blessing, i've consistently fasted. Fasting became a consistent practice when I experienced his glory and grace after refraining from food. I'm currently on a 21 day fast now and just on day 3 I received a miraculous breakthrough on something i've been praying and waiting on for 3 years. 3 years of toiling, crying and praying and in 3 days I get a breakthrough. I was blown away.

I know for a fact it was something that the devil did not want me to have. I've learned that when God says yes, nothing else matters but I couldn't receive it until I leveled up in my anointing. Fasting enlarges your capacity for faith and helps remove those stubborn demons that regular prayer can't destroy. Ever wonder why you can't get the victory over certain things in your life even though you're praying. Increase and intensify your anointing by denying food when you pray. It's a tremendous weapon to the believer and a great way to hear from the lord. Do you need answers on what to do in life? Who to be with and where to live? Fast, worship and seek him and he'll give you all the answers you need. Once you're obedient to the things of him, he'll prosper you in mighty ways.

> *And Jesus rebuked the demon, and it came out of him, and the boy was cured instantly. 19) Then the disciples came to Jesus and asked privately, Why could we not drive it out? 20) He said to them, Because of the littleness of your faith [that is, your lack of firmly relying trust]. For truly I say to you, if you have faith [that is living] like a grain of mustard seed, you can say to this mountain, Move from here to yonder place, and it will move; and nothing will be impossible to you. 21) But this kind does not go out except by prayer and fasting. (Matthew 17: 18- 21,Amp)*

So what Jesus is saying here, is some demons are stubborn and can't be cast out normally. You must be dedicated to a committed fast and worship process in order to rid yourself of those demonic attacks that just won't let up. When it comes to being victorious over the enemy, you must be willing to be disciplined, sacrifice and pray in the spirit. Learn how to intercede for your family and for this world when others can't pray for themselves. Your prayers could make all the difference to the body of christ worldwide. We live in a dangerous world where destruction, disease, famine, racism, hate and fear are destroying humanity globally. We need unity and we need bold and courageous prayer warriors to rise up and say what needs to be said and do what needs to be done. We need more word temples teaching biblical ministry and raising up a new generation of bold believers.

We need to use all media platforms and technology to promote the Gospel and share Gods love. The world cries for unashamed believers who will lift him up in glory. Bold enough to share the teachings of Jesus and tell the truth about what the bible says. Strong enough to be a witness and let our own light, be an example of how cool and awesome salvation can be. It's time to stop being concerned with being politically correct and focus on winning as many souls as possible. Why are there so many churches on every corner but so much corruption in the world? Let's get out of the church and go into the world like Jesus did, meet people in the streets and marketplace.

Take every opportunity you can when having conversations. We must be unafraid of standing out and being different from everybody else. If you really think about it, we are the ones the world should want to be like. We need to speak the truth and share the gospel in a loving and fun way and show folks that this life is more rewarding than they could ever imagine.

God is able to do the impossible in your life. He can bring you out of the darkest dungeons and sparkle you in the warm light of the sun. He knows how to clean you up and help you start over. The bible also known as the Believers Instruction Before Leaving Earth is a guide to show you how to make it in this world. It shows you how to defeat your enemies and receive all the wins and blessings he has for you. It teaches us how to take authority and dominion over this earth and over circumstances. It reveals how he really feels about you and how much he loves you unconditionally. Whether you consider yourself a good or bad person or no matter if you've done some terrible things in your life. God will never stop loving you.

People might but he'll never turn his back on you and he's the only one you can truly count on. He loves all sinners and he's patiently waiting for us all to get it right by surrendering to his will. Real people who remember where God brought them from in their own sin are more compassionate and waiting with open arms. Trust in the Lord but know there are good people out there who are compassionate and operating in pure love. We're here to give you hugs and the truth about the anointing.

> *It is better to trust and take refuge in the Lord than to put*
> *confidence in man. (Psalm 118:8. Amp.)*

Step 8: Fast, Pray and Have Faith To Be A Miracle Magnet.

Side Note: This New Generation Of Believers Will Change The World.

When I Pray, I Slay

Confess to one another therefore your faults (your slips, your false steps, your offenses, your sins) and pray [also] for one another, that you may be healed and restored [to a spiritual tone of mind and heart]. The earnest (heartfelt, continued) prayer of a righteous man makes tremendous power available [dynamic in its working]. (James 5:16, Amp)

Don't underestimate the power of prayer because it gives voice to our needs. Prayers are our petitions before God for the things we need. It's not about the results of the person praying but rather the fact of praying to God almighty.

That's worshipping and trusting him to deal with your needs. You're acknowledging that fact that you need his help and you can't do it without him. It's an invitation to enter into Gods presence because he hears your prayers. You get so much insight and wisdom from our father when you enter into his presence. It's like sitting at the feet of Jesus and soaking in all the wisdom and knowledge he has for you to live a life of victory. We're able to intercede for our families, children and even the world just by entering into worship and allowing your heart to be touched.

Your prayers being answered are not based on any eloquent elaborate prayers and words. That means nothing to him because he already knows what you need before you to come to him anyway. He just wants your willing heart and for you to trust and rest in him. He doesn't like when we pray out loud to try to impress people because he's knows its fake.

> *And when you pray, do not heap up phrases (multiply words, repeating the same ones over and over) as the Gentiles do, for they think they will be heard for their much speaking. 8) Do not be like them, for your Father knows what you need before you ask Him. (Matthew 6:7-8, Amp.)*

Victory Over Your Enemies

There are specific prayers in the bible about defeating your enemies if you're under spiritual attacks. Pray these specific prayers daily and you'll see results and learn how to beat the devil at his own game. Remember the devils power is very limited. He's a spirit full of bad habits and characteristics and he needs a body in order to operate anything tangible in the earth. This consist of speaking it, believing and expecting. If you resist him and rebuke him, he will flee.

Don't give him a body and don't give him a mind to control. In other words don't fall for his tricks. Don't let him use people to bait you into arguments, bad decisions or ungodly relationships. Nothing can touch you, if you're not a willing participant. Stay in the word and feed your heart faith prayers daily to stay strong.

> *The Lord has heard my supplication; the Lord receives my prayer. 10) Let all my enemies be ashamed and sorely troubled; let them turn back and be put to shame suddenly. (Psalm 6: 9-10 Amp)*

Healing

There are scriptures teaching you how to bring healing into your life. You don't have to struggle with sickness, poverty, afflictions or disease.

You don't have to wrestle with your finances or fight with demons. That's called toiling. The opposite of that is living in rest and peace. This means to give it to God to deal with and rest and be assured that he will work it out for you. Calm down, exhale, pray, release and rest.

> *Is anyone among you sick? He should call in the church elders (the spiritual guides).*
> *And they should pray over him, anointing him with oil in the Lord's name.*
> *15) And the prayer [that is] of faith will save him who is sick, and the Lord will*
> *restore him; and if he has committed sins, he will be forgiven. (James 5:14-15, Amp)*

Holy Oil

Do you have any bless oil? Get a small bottle of pure olive oil and pray over it in the name of Jesus. It then becomes a powerful and spiritual symbol and weapon of warfare. It had great biblical significance then and it does now. When you go into your prayer closet, get your oil and rub a cross on the forehead of yourself, your children, doorways, windows and even body parts. This elevates and renders powerful prayers and results.

> *And they drove out many unclean spirits and anointed with oil many who*
> *were sick and cured them. (Mark 6:13, Amp) Is anyone among you sick? He*
> *should call in the church elders (the spiritual guides). And they should pray over*
> *him, anointing him with oil in the Lord's name. (James 5:14, Amp)*

Once you create your bottle of olive oil, pray this prayer and use it daily for miraculous results.

Prayer to Anoint Your Oil

Heavenly Father, I pray the anointing over this holy oil. This oil speaks of the perfection of your finished work. I declare that wherever this oil is applied, it will bring praise and glory to your name. Lord we pray against danger and evil spirits and thank you for your unlimited protection over our families. Let the walls of my house hear the word of God and be blessed in Jesus Name, Amen.

Prayer To Receive Gods Promises

The Prayer of Jabez

Jabez cried to the God of Israel, saying, Oh, that You would bless me and enlarge my border, and that Your hand might be with me, and You would keep me from evil so it might not hurt me! And God granted his request. (1 Chronicles 4:10 Amp)

Jabez was humble and acknowledged God as the lord of his life. He's not just speaking of physical land but he wanted his spiritual territory to be increased to claim generations for the lord of Israel. He knew that would impact the kingdom of God more effectively. He wanted the way God saw him to be increased because he knew that would change everything else for him. The name Jabez means "born of pain" and he asked to be relieved of his pain. This is a very powerful prayer that I try to pray everyday. Pray this everyday for a week and you'll get some phenomenal breakthroughs.

Be specific but sincere about your prayers and let God do the rest. Pray this prayer.

MIRACLE PRAYER

Heavenly Father, help me to see myself the way you see me. Give me certainty and integrity and show me my destiny and what you've called me to do. Don't let me be overwhelmed by difficult task, but let the holy spirit guide me with ease, confidence and anointing. Bring my enemies to swift justice. Increase my hands as I walk into this season of Boldness, Power and Strength. I'm highly favored of the lord. I'm a world overcomer. Lord I know you never intended for me to struggle that's why I'm crowned with Glory & Honor. Greater is he that's in me than he that's in the world. Divine protection and anointing is upon me like a shield everywhere I go. Favor over takes me in all that i do. I'm independent of this worlds systems and I only rely on my father to meet my needs and my storehouse is in excess. I'm living in the overflow of your blessings and lack comes no where near me, in Jesus name, Amen.

Financial Increase Prayer

Thank You Jesus for financing my business and giving me money making ideas. Thank You father that i'm debt free and I thank you for the wisdom to solve my problems. Sharpen my mind and give me brilliant strategies in business in Jesus name, Amen.

Step 9: Prayer Is A Powerful Weapon

Side Note: Don't Pray Weak Prayers Unless You Want Weak Results.

Taking Dominion & Authority

Dominion: Rulership, Territory, Sovereign Authority,
the Power or Right of Governing and Controlling

In the bible the Dominion of God refers to complete ownership and supremacy which includes the heavens, hell and physical universe. He has gifted us the Authority and Dominion over the entire earth. He has given us the word to show us how to release the anointing and the blessings. The anointing is the power of God on you to do something. Jesus paid the price to make us all righteous and reign as kings on this earth. So you can't live like a peasant and a king at the same time. You must choose.

For if because of one man's trespass (lapse, offense) death reigned through that one, much more surely will those who receive [God's] overflowing grace (unmerited favor) and the free gift of righteousness [putting them into right standing with Himself] reign as kings in life through the one Man Jesus Christ (the Messiah, the Anointed One). (Romans 5:17 Amp)

Now let's talk about the significance of living in that power and authority and understanding your dominion mandate. Words are the tools that God gives us to call things into existence. We must not underestimate the power of speaking to things in our lives that need to be shifted or removed permanently. A perfect example of taking authority is speaking to the mountains in your life and commanding them to disappear. Kings and

Queens are not timid in the face of adversity, they just take control over something and rule it.

Truly I tell you, whoever says to this mountain, Be lifted up and thrown into the sea! and does not doubt at all in his heart but believes that what he says will take place, it will be done for him. (Mark 11:23 Amp)

Nothing shall be impossible unto you so just speak what you want. Speak the results and believe it. That's an incredible greatness for the believers of christ. We have supernatural authority over our circumstances and we don't have to just settle for anything that's done to us. You must speak blessings of increase over your business, your job and your family.

Environments change when you walk in and people are blessed by your presence everywhere you go. You have the kind of greatness over you that blesses and delivers people you prayed for. You must be able to release the power thats been placed inside of you. You must believe and say what the word of God says. Then you must cancel doubt and release the anointing of God over your possessions. We were designed to show the world what God is like. We are to be his representatives of what life in Christ looks like.

We must redeem our dominion in a fallen world and not accept the normalcy. We are not normal and God has set us apart from everyone else. We can't do everything they do, therefore we don't get the same results they get. We decree, release and expect while they fear, worry and sink in defeat. We speak to the mountains and pray in the spirit while they run from the devil or join his army.

As I stated earlier we have a foot in two worlds, the spirit world and the natural. We need to be able to understand how to operate in the spirit world in such a way that it affects the natural. Your spiritual life is more important to focus on than the natural because what goes on in your spirit translates into your flesh. What's on the inside shows up in your actions on the outside. When you understand the power that's been given to us, you'll gain confidence and increased faith and take back everything that's yours.

You're not supposed to be broke, sick or dealing with lack and all sorts of foolish attacks. But you will if you don't know any better. If your don't realize who you are in Christ and learn to harness your authority you will suffer in defeat all the time. Here's what Paul said in Ephesians.

[For I always pray to] the God of our Lord Jesus Christ, the Father of glory, that He may grant you a spirit of wisdom and revelation [of insight into mysteries and secrets] in the [deep and intimate] knowledge of Him. 18) By having the eyes of your heart flooded with light, so that you can know and understand the hope to which He has called you, and how rich is His glorious inheritance in the saints (His set-apart ones).(Ephesians 1:17-18, Amp)

How powerful is this mighty word from the lord. Believe and receive and study those scriptures. Refer to this book as your daily guide when you're feeling weak and weary and the enemy is trying to break you down. That's one of his number one tactics of war is making you weary and tired. He constantly rides your back and tries to overwhelm you with test after test and storm after storm. He wants you to give up, fall into depression and be so exhausted that you don't open your bible or go to church.

The devil is a liar. This is the very time to run to the altar, take an intercessory prayer class and combat those negative emotions. Watch sermons on youtube and keep this book with you at all times. Enough is enough because you now identify all of his tactics. Now that you know the play, make your move. Stand tall, straighten your back and you will come out of this in no time. Remember you are only empowered through your union with God.

That's what makes you strong and will determine your success. You are weak alone and will never accomplish anything that will last, without God. Draw your strength from him because thats where we get our might.

Put on the whole armor of God because the enemy is studying you and knows just how to attack you. You must be fitly clothed in your armor and armed with effective weapons of destruction. You must have confidence that it's already done by God according to his word. You don't have to constantly beg him for the same things and pray the same prayers daily. Believe it's already done and thank him for that and for what he's presently doing. It's imperative that you stand on the finished works of Jesus and go claim your blessings in Jesus name.

In conclusion, be strong in the Lord [be empowered through your union with Him]; draw your strength from Him [that strength which His boundless might provides]. 11) Put on God's whole armor [the armor of a heavy-armed soldier which God supplies], that you may be able successfully to stand up against [all] the strategies and the deceits of the devil. 12) For we are not wrestling with flesh and blood [contending only with physical opponents], but against the despotisms, against the powers, against [the master spirits who are] the world rulers of this present darkness, against the spirit forces of wickedness in the heavenly (supernatural) sphere. 13) Therefore put on God's complete armor, that you may be able to resist and stand your ground on the evil day [of danger], and, having done all [the crisis demands], to stand [firmly in your place]. (Ephesians 6: 10-13 Amp)

Step 10: Identify The Significance of Your Authority and Use It.

Side Note: Never Let Your Enemies See You Sweat or They'll Pounce.

ACKNOWLEDGEMENTS

Thank you Heavenly Father for all your marvelous works. You indeed are the Great I Am. I'm humbled by this opportunity to share your love with the world. Thank you for not giving up on me until I saw myself through your eyes.Thank You for choosing me even though I'm not worthy. You waited just for me and prepared a table before me in the presence of my antagonist. You are Amazing and Supreme in all ways.

To my phenomenal children who have been my constant motivation and inspiration in life. You are my greatest teachers and blessings. Thank You for being awesome, hilarious beings. Thank you for your encouragement and for always telling me, "you can do it mom". I'm excited about what God is doing in each of your lives and how you'll one day take Dominion over the earth and represent for Christ. I will be by your side to the very end lifting you up no matter what.

Thank You to all my family and friends who sincerely had my back always and forever, I'll treasure you. I pray Gods best over your lives daily. I acknowledge you and call you into an awakened state of mind and encourage you to infuse the power of God in your hearts. You will feel an immediate shift and you'll never be the same.

Sending Light and Joy your way.

God Bless The World Shalom

GLOSSARY

Anointing: is the power of God on you to accomplish something. It gives you unusual abilities

Abundance: a large quantity or volume of something

Authority: jurisdiction, control, dominance

Awakening: an act of waking from sleep, a moment of becoming suddenly aware of something, coming into existence or awareness.

Covenant: an agreement, pledge, commitment, promise

Defeat: beat, ruin, derail, reject, overthrow, dismiss, hinder

Depression: unhappiness, sadness, sorrow, despair, misery, gloom, low spirits

Discernment: The ability to judge well

Dominion: Jurisdiction, supremacy, Authority, Rulership, right to govern and control

Faith: is the connection between God and Man. It's the complete belief and total dependence on Gods help and not on logical reasoning.

Favor: kindness, preferred treatment

Grace: Favor, approval, regard

Mandate: An order or decree, authorization to establish a territory

Repentance: regret for sin or wrong doing

Roars: a full, deep, prolonged cry uttered by a Lion

Royalty: Sovereign, majestic lineage

Miracle: wonder, divine phenomenon, sensation

Satanic Attack: spiritual strategies from satan to destroy your life

Strongholds: satanic forces that keep the unbeliever captive or incapacitated and exalts itself against the truth of God

Supernatural: superhuman, extraordinary, unearthly, unnatural

Unconscious: insensible, dormant, unaware, suppressed.

Unyoked: difference in beliefs in christ and worship, not as one

Victory: overcoming an enemy or antagonist

Weary: tired, exhausted, worn out

Scriptures from Amplified Version. Classic Edition

NOTES

NOTES

NOTES

NOTES

NOTES

NOTES

NOTES

Printed in the United States
By Bookmasters